Sarah Bartlett is is a professional astrologer and author of internationally bestselling books such as *The Little Book of Moon Magic*, *The Tarot Bible*, *The Witch's Spellbook*, *The Secrets of the Universe in 100 Symbols* and *National Geographic Guide to the World's Supernatural Places*. Sarah practises natural magic, tarot, astrology and other esoteric arts in the heart of the countryside.

The
Little
Book *of*
Practical
Magic

Sarah Bartlett

PIATKUS

PIATKUS

First published in Great Britain in 2018 by Piatkus
This hardback edition published in Great Britain in 2022 by Piatkus

1 3 5 7 9 10 8 6 4 2

A CIP catalogue record for this book
is available from the British Library.

ISBN 978-0-349-41941-1

Typeset in Perpetua by M Rules
Printed and bound in Great Britain by
Clays Ltd, Elcograf S.p.A

Papers used by Piatkus are from well-managed forests
and other responsible sources.

Piatkus
An imprint of
Little, Brown Book Group
Carmelite House
50 Victoria Embankment
London EC4Y 0DZ

An Hachette UK Company
www.hachette.co.uk

www.littlebrown.co.uk

To Jess, and all the other magicians in my life.

Acknowledgements

With many thanks to everyone at Piatkus for their magical support, and to my agent, Chelsey Fox, for over twenty years of friendship.

Contents

Introduction 1

1 How to Start Using Magic 7

2 Auras and Chakras – the Magic
  Within Ourselves 49

3 Spells and Enchantments 73

4 Psychic Protection, Sixth Sense
  and Dream Interpretation 117

5 The Magic of Divination 163

6 Using the Tarot, Palmistry and
  Numerology 212

Conclusion 263

Introduction

My first experience of magic was when I was a child and lived in Malaysia. A lovely Chinese lady taught me how to protect myself from negative people and situations, and how to understand the magic of the universe. At the weekends, my father and I used to go beachcombing on the east coast, which in those days was still quite wild and untouched. Just the place itself was magical. We weren't sure what we were looking for; we were just looking. Although the beaches were mostly fine sand, I came across two white crystal-like stones, and when we returned to our home in Kuala Lumpur, the Chinese lady told me that they were of 'great benefit to those who deserve their power'. She placed them in the south-east corner of our home and told me that we would soon be prosperous. It wasn't long until our lives changed for the better and we returned to England. Later, when I was going through my first relationship break-up, I used to hold these crystals and wish that the universe would send me gentle love but also a passionate life. When it obliged, I realised that the stones on the beach were alive with their own special magic. My two stones are my friends. They still remain on my desk, and I hold them whenever I feel I need a deeper connection to the universe.

This book contains such magic.

What is magic?

Magic is simply about making wondrous and good things happen, and with this practical guide you can quickly learn to make magic in your life and to enhance your own intuitive healing powers.

Magic is based on a very simple formula. The ancient alchemist's phrase 'As above, so below' describes that what we see up there in the sky – the constellations and the planets – reflects what or who we are down here on earth, and so on. In fact, we are all One. We could say we are one and the same as the universe, and what we see up there *is* us. This universal energy pervades all things, whether you call it divine or cosmic. Known as ch'i (or qi) in Taoist philosophy – or prana in Indian cultures – this energy permeates and animates everything, from a lion to a stone. By correspondence or association, when we practise magic we put similar energies at work together. In magic, we use the words 'correspondence' or 'association' a lot. They mean that certain symbols, energies or qualities relate to one another. By using these associated or corresponding ingredients, thoughts, spells or tools, we maximise the power of the spell. This amplifies, boosts and enhances specific energies that we want to flow out from us and back to us.

Whether these energies are colours, images, crystals or other symbols, you are sending out enriched and boosted desires or wishes to the universe, and what you send out usually comes back to you threefold (according to the law of magic) – or tenfold if you're lucky!

Simply put, your intention to manifest a dream or achieve a goal is amplified by using ingredients and/or exercises that correspond to that desire.

That is the beauty of magic.

Types of magic

You're going to use a selection of magical methods in this book. Here are some of the main ones that I've included:

1. Natural magic
Using candles, herbs, plants, crystals and other ingredients in spells, you can enhance and direct energy for positive results.

2. Sympathetic magic
This is when you use objects, colour or placements to represent your specific desire and its outcome; for example, you might place a red crystal (red signifies achievement and success) in the south part of your home to boost your desire for fame – and be rewarded.

3. Folk magic
Here, you use old superstitions and practices, such as using a mirror to see your future husband.

4. Divination magic
The magic of seeing how to live your life in the future is known as divination magic. This works by using specific

tools, such as the tarot, to help you connect to universal knowledge about past, present and future.

5. Healing magic
This is when you work with chakras, aura and intuition, combined with the universal energy, to promote holistic healing and psychic or spiritual oneness. This also covers how you interpret your dreams to understand more about your psyche or unconscious world.

6. High magic
You utilise high magic when you perform rituals (using natural magic ingredients plus, perhaps, calling on a deity to help) and you chant your spell out loud.

Why magic?

Some people say that we can't change fate and that it's written in the stars. But then, the stars are always evolving; they are not as static as was once believed. Think also of what is written in the stars as being like your signature. Supposedly, that too is fixed, but have you never changed your signature? Have you never changed one letter to make the signature better, more legible, or more stylish? Well, it's the same with your destiny. Now, you can learn how to tweak it with the help of magic to make your life more fulfilling and rewarding.

Magic is about living a life where you take control of your destiny. Destiny is what you make of your life;

it's the melting pot of your choices and who you are, mingled with the encounters or influences you meet on your way. Strangely, we are often led down paths we believe we haven't consciously chosen but somehow were led to without knowing how or why. This can be the magic of the universe calling us, telling us that we have to follow this road, because for some reason it is part of our personal journey. So, be led, but don't become 'a stray'.

Always make a conscious choice for your decisions, because when you start to engage in the power of your own magic, this is where fate and free will merge to make love, life, or whatever it is you truly want, become real for you.

How to use this book

Full of charms, spells and potions, this book can help you to discover not only the secrets of herbs, fortune telling, divination and psychic power, but also how to work with them for personal success, love and well-being. Along with the many other magical ways to live our lives, this book includes the simple art of crystal placement, and other ways to use crystals to enhance your life.

Use this book in many ways. You can dip in and out when you want to find spells or recipes for love or success. You can read it from front to back and immerse yourself in the wonders of a magical life. Alternatively, you can be more specific and discover the power of divination, dreams or your aura. Of course, you can just stick to the fun side of working with spells, crystals and the tarot. Enjoy a magical lifestyle now, because everything you need to know to create one is included in this little book.

Chapter 1

How to Start Using Magic

This chapter and Chapter 2 form a basic guide to the magical ingredients you can use to help you amplify and enhance your own innate magical powers. By using these ingredients and their related symbols, and by awakening and healing your own hidden force field – your aura – you will begin to see amazing results. Whether it's to enhance your love life or your sensuality, or to protect your home or attract success and prosperity, all the ingredients included here will help you to achieve your desires.

This chapter includes:

- The Toolkit basics
- The Toolkit crystals – what they mean and how to use them
- Common plants and herbs for healing – their meaning and use
- The planets, sun, moon and seasons
- Deities

You will also be using auras and chakras, as explained in Chapter 2.

The Toolkit – basics

All the things you need to use for magical healing work and harmonious living are usually close at hand. You don't have to kit yourself out with special effects or unusual items. The good news is that there are no wands, altars, cauldrons or broomsticks involved. This first chapter introduces you to the various magical ingredients that are naturally out there in the world. Whether they are herbs, trees, crystals or colours, it is the energy of yourself, combined with the energy of everything around you, that will invoke magic in your life.

Another useful magical aid is to work on auspicious days of the seasons (the cycles of the earth and the earth's relation to the sun and the universe are integral parts of making magic) – that's why many magical rituals and spells are performed on specific days, such as the summer solstice or spring equinox.

I have also included a smattering of Greek deities to call on, because drawing on their symbolic power can amplify our magical results. Why? Because gods and goddesses are rich motifs in our collective psyche, and in various embodiments they are deeply embedded in all civilisations throughout the world. They are also symbols of the planetary energies themselves. These symbolic motifs continue to be part of our culture, and so remain, albeit usually hidden, within your deepest unconscious self. You carry these archetypes within you, and when you bring these deities alive, you can work their magic right into your life; for example, there's a simple way to work with vain Venus's seductive energy to bring you new love – so why not give it a try? (See page 78.)

Getting started with your Toolkit

There is no set magic pack, but here is a simple list of things to get you started, which no white magician or healer would be without. These objects are not expensive, and you may even already have them to hand.

Crystals

A simple set of crystals can be used for spells and rituals or for divination.

Their benefits are:

- Crystals can be laid out in certain patterns to provide healing power.
- You can meditate on a crystal to manifest a dream.
- Placing certain crystals in the home can provide protection and benefit.
- Stones can be put under the pillow for good sleep or for dreams to come true.
- Many crystals are used in spells (see the spells section starting on page 73).

The main crystals for your Toolkit are:

- White quartz (preferably one that is small enough to carry with you, and one pointed at each end, known as a double terminator) – to manifest or amplify power
- Rose quartz, pink tourmaline or ruby – for love
- Smoky quartz – for protection
- Onyx – for grounding ideas and balancing energy
- Tiger's eye – for creativity and passion
- Turquoise – for adventure and travel
- Pearl or moonstone – to enhance feelings and to know the truth
- Citrine – for prosperity, wealth and success
- Lapis lazuli – for spiritual and emotional healing

Detailed information on each crystal starts on page 19.

Herbs

Herbs and other plants have long been used by magical healers, both for their natural medicinal properties and also their magical attributes. These herbs are an essential ingredient in your magic kitchen.

Their uses include:

- Dried herbs can be used in potions, carried in a pouch or sprinkled in secret places to promote prosperity, love or success.
- Some herbs can be brewed into infusions or teas and drunk to promote inner healing.

- Essential oils (which are made from plants) are used for beauty potions, spells and enchantments.
- Add essential oils to your bathing routine to enhance self-confidence.

The herbs and oils best suited for magic work are listed below; choose from the following, but don't assume you have to keep them all in your cupboard. Further details on meaning and uses start on page 34.

- Lavender (petals, dried flowers and essential oil)
- Rosemary (dried leaves, fresh leaves)
- Basil (dried leaves, fresh plant)
- Thyme (dried leaves, fresh plant or oil)
- Rose (petals, rose water or essential oil)
- Sandalwood (essential oil or incense)
- Cinnamon (fresh spice or incense)
- Cedar (essential oil or incense)
- Jasmine (oil or fresh petals)
- Ginger (fresh or dried)
- Ylang ylang (essential oil)

General tools
Candles Have one or two each of white, pink, red, yellow, blue, green and black candles in your Toolkit.

Candles generally amplify and open up energy, and can be lit and used in rituals and spells, or they can be left unlit and, depending on the colour, placed in various locations in the home to invoke empowerment and confidence. (Remember: never leave a burning candle unattended.)

- **White** candles are used in many spells to invoke purity and calm, but they also symbolise strength and vision.
- **Pink** candles can be used in love spells and enchantments. Placed by the entrance to your home, they will also welcome romance into your life.
- **Red** is the colour of passion; using red candles in healing or spell work will enhance all aspects of love and sexuality.
- Placing a **yellow** candle on your desk instils good communication and can bring you new contacts in business dealings.
- **Blue** candles can be included in chakra healing (see page 61) to help you become more aware of your spiritual or soul self.

The problem with scented candles

Don't buy scented candles. They may appear to combine the colour and the scent you might require, by association, but they are usually chemically based and not magic-friendly; however, some spells may ask you to drip an essential oil over the candle before lighting it.

- Use **green** candles in magic work associated with prosperity, grounding ideas or manifesting goals.

- **Black** candles are useful for psychic and chakra protection.

A mirror You can use either a large mirror propped up on your mantelpiece, with space in front of it for placing various magical objects, or a small mirror resting against a wall.

Mirrors are used to amplify energy, and they will double the energy of everything you see reflected in the glass. Placed behind a lit candle, a mirror can enhance spells and the use of divination tools.

Good-quality paper to use for writing down spells or for numerology work.

Use either real parchment paper if you can find it, or good-quality, acid-free paper, which will enhance the power of the natural world embodied within.

Paper is a natural ingredient in your Toolkit. Each enchantment that requires a written rhyme or invocation will work better if it is written on a separate sheet of paper. The spell or magic works because it has its own unique energy and place.

A journal or notebook to keep notes and ideas, and to record results of spell work and/or divination results.

Divination tools

For this book you need the following:

- A deck of tarot cards (see Chapter 6 for more information).
- The 12 zodiac crystals, or as many of them as you can collect (see page 21).

The Toolkit crystals

Let's now discover the fabulous glamour of crystal power and how it can instantly bring magic into your life.

What are crystals?

Crystals are formed from the molten magma and fiery gases and liquids that penetrate the earth's crust. When these substances meet solid rock, they form a range of different structures known as crystals. Some have been created by the forces of water, others by hot liquids or cooling magma which penetrate fissures in the bedrock. Other crystals are created by slower processes due to geological stresses and movements in the earth's crust. Some take hundreds of years to form, such as amethyst, whereas others such as obsidian are formed very quickly in a matter of days.

How do they work?

Every crystal has an internal molecular structure, which, although seeming to be a piece of inert rock, is in fact very much alive. This internal structure creates a vibrational frequency, which is called the piezoelectric effect and was discovered by the French chemist Pierre Curie (1859–1906). That sounds a bit technical, but, simply put, when you hold a crystal tightly in your hand the mechanical pressure creates a voltage that brings the electromagnetic force or vibrational frequency to life. This effect is reversible, and if the polarity of the voltage is altered – for example when your tight squeeze is changed to an open fist – the crystal's electromagnetic force alternates: in other words, it expands and contracts. It is alive with energy. This is the basis of how quartz watches work.

Crystal history

- Red garnets were set in shields, buckles and sword hilts by ancient Sumerian warriors as protective talismans.
- In Hindu and Vedic religions, moonstones were thought to be drops of moonbeams.
- The Romans believed that clear quartz crystal was water frozen by the gods and they carried a piece to keep their hands cool.
- Lapis lazuli was prized by the ancient Egyptians as a symbol of the heavens and the power of the gods.
- Rubies were laid beneath the foundations of ancient Chinese and East Asian buildings to secure good fortune to the structure and its inhabitants.

Caring for and dedicating your crystals

Choosing crystals is fun, and you may feel drawn to one or two in particular as you browse in a local crystal shop. Alternatively, you can buy them online – but do take care that you buy from a specialist supplier, because there are many fake crystals out there.

Once crystals become your companions, you need to care and look after them as you would your friends. Crystals, unless worn, carried or regularly held, or put in places around the home for specific magic work, are best kept in a silk scarf in a drawer to protect them from damage – or even negative energy from certain visitors.

Crystal cleansing

You might also need to cleanse your stone of any geopathic stress (see also page 18) or negative energy that it might have picked up from others on its long route from the depths of the earth to your home.

Use either natural spring water, purified water or, if you're lucky to live nearby, the water from a flowing high-mountain stream. Try to avoid tap water, but if you can't get a bottle of spring water, tap water is better than nothing.

1. Fill a glass bowl with water and place your crystals in the bowl.
2. As you put each one in the bowl, say: 'With this water you are now purified and cleansed of any negative energy.'
3. Leave the crystals in the water overnight, if possible under a full moon (the power of the moon influences

tides, so think what it can do with your bowl of water).
4. The next day, let the crystals dry off naturally on a window ledge, before putting them in a safe place, preferably wrapped in a silk scarf in a box, or place them and use them as required for your magic work.

Crystal dedication

When you first take your crystal home, you might also like to dedicate it with the intention for positive healing energy to flow through it and for it to be the focus of the goodness of the universe. Here's how:

1. Take your crystal in your hand, hold it tightly and close your eyes. Relax.
2. As you feel its energy in your fist, imagine a cloak of white light enveloping you both. The light is the light of the universe, and as it holds you in its embrace, feel it protecting both yourself and the crystal.
3. Repeat this dedication three times: 'The light of the universe is giving protection to us both so that this crystal will always be used for the highest good.'
4. Put the crystal back in its silk scarf or place of honour in the home, and you will begin to feel a real sense of affinity to its powers.

Using crystals

Crystals can be used in the following ways:

- Placed in the home to create harmony and to restore balance.

- For divination techniques (see Chapter 5).
- To carry with you for self-empowerment.
- To wear as jewellery – for attracting positivity.
- For chakra healing, balancing and aura well-being (see Chapter 2).
- For spells and rituals for all kinds of magical work (see Chapter 3).
- To give psychic protection – to deflect negative energy from others (see Chapter 4).
- To protect against geopathic stress (that is, electricity power lines overhead and underground, dysfunctional ley lines, geological fault lines, underground cavities, subterranean water courses that have been blocked or re-routed, and so on – all this creates negativity in our world). Once cleansed when newly purchased they have a protective power for the future.
- For dream work – to help sleep and to dream well (see Chapter 4).

Like many things in magic, colours, crystals, astrological signs of the zodiac, deities, herbs, chakras and auras all correspond to one another, and this energises and enhances different emotions, ideas and feelings in ourselves. You don't have to learn what these all are to be a successful magic healer, but it's useful to know the basics, and you can quickly learn these by seeing how certain crystals and their colours link to particular signs of the zodiac, as listed on page 21.

The six main crystals – what they mean and how to use them

You will find spells and rituals for using these six main crystals later, but with the following information you can adapt them to your own magical needs, too. They are such captivating stones – pretty, beguiling and glamorous – but yes, they do have this intrinsic magical power, so why not make use of it?

WHITE QUARTZ

Uses: general manifesting or amplifying power

Main qualities: white quartz reveals true desires and promotes success. It is a crystal that can be used to boost the power of other crystals. I often keep a double terminator (a crystal pointed at both ends) on my mantelpiece to generate positive energy throughout the home.

ROSE QUARTZ

Uses: for love, romance

Main qualities: rose quartz softens the heart, enhances romantic attachments and attracts others to you when worn or carried. It can be used in many spells to bring new love into your life, restore emotional trust or create a harmonious atmosphere.

SMOKY QUARTZ

Uses: a general stone of protection

Main qualities: smoky quartz protects you from negative people and negative thinking and brings you down to earth about your true needs or desires. When worn or carried, it can also protect you from geopathic stress in the environment as well as being a source of psychic protection.

RED CARNELIAN

Uses: for focus, creativity, luck and passion

Main qualities: red carnelian stimulates all the senses when worn or carried (yes, even the sexiest ones). It is a perfect companion to promote passion, a love of life, creative ideas, and determination and luck to achieve your current goal.

SUNSTONE

Uses: for prosperity, wealth and success

Main qualities: sunstone is the queen of stones for all forms of abundance, whether for an abundance of career opportunities or wealthy ambition. Don't leave home without this crystal in your pocket, or you can wear it discreetly, of course. Why discretion? Because sunstone is a brilliant golden-coloured pal that could outshine you in the market place, encouraging other people to feel brash and confident in its presence. When used discreetly, however, it will boost your own inner richness and attract outer riches towards you.

LAPIS LAZULI

Uses: spiritual and emotional healing

Main qualities: lapis lazuli is a stone for harmonious living and loving. It amplifies truth (in all forms) but it also brings self-awareness and a direct connection to universal or divine energy. Does this sound far out? Well, in ancient Colombian America, it was believed to have come from the starry night itself and embodied all the gods of the heavens, so get wearing this exquisite stone and draw all the powers of the universe towards you.

The 12 magic crystals

From the following 12 stones, choose your own zodiac crystal to add to your six main crystals. If you also manage to collect all the others, you'll be ready to bewitch, entrance, enrapture and charm others to enhance all forms of love, success and happiness in your personal world.

Aries – ruby (rich or bright red)
Taurus – emerald (intense or vibrant green)
Gemini – citrine (lemon yellow)
Cancer – moonstone (opaque white/soft blue)
Leo – tiger's eye (burnt yellow/umber)
Virgo – peridot (soft green)
Libra – blue sapphire (pale blue/white)
Scorpio – obsidian (black)
Sagittarius – turquoise (turquoise green or blue)
Capricorn – garnet (dark purple/red)
Aquarius – amber (orange)
Pisces – amethyst (purple/violet)

For each sign of the zodiac, keywords, symbols plus the crystal's legend and qualities are given below. There is also a brief magical 'tip' for using the crystal whatever sign you are.

ARIES

21 March–19 April
Crystal: ruby
Symbol: the ram
Element: fire
Colour: red
Keywords: action, impulse, drive, sexual desire

Legend Whether worn to banish evil, promote lust or ward off the plague, the ruby was prized by kings and royalty, and from the ancient cultures of the Far East to medieval Europe it carried a higher price tag than a diamond.

Qualities The ruby's intense carmine red is associated with fire, passion and action, and is at the heart of the stone's ability to empower you with its volatile energy. This stone not only enhances enthusiasm, drive and desire, but when placed in the home, or on your desk at work, it also inspires you and others to get things done.

Abracadabra Carry a ruby with you to boost your courage, or to prove a point.

TAURUS

20 April –20 May
Crystal: emerald
Symbol: the bull
Element: earth
Colour: green
Keywords: patience, care, tenacity, compassion

Legend The ancient Egyptians believed that the emerald was a symbol of eternal life, and for the Aztec and Inca peoples, emeralds held secrets and divine messages from the gods. One Chinese legend states that wearing emeralds on a Thursday would promote good health and prosperity.

Qualities Like the sign of Taurus, the vibrant-green emerald embodies faith, loyalty and infinite love. Emeralds amplify your harmonious approach to life and love, and wearing the stone can bring long-lasting unity and peace with others. Worn or carried, it can attract new love to you, and will also boost creativity and mental clarity.

Abracadabra Place the stone under your pillow to promote restful sleep and sweet dreams.

GEMINI

21 May–20 June
Crystal: citrine
Symbol: the twins
Element: air
Colour: zingy yellow
Keywords: versatility, communication,
   optimism, joy

Legend The Renaissance German metallurgist George Bauer renamed the stone, a form of clear bright-yellow quartz, after the Latin word for a lemon, *citron*. Although often confused with topaz, citrine became a popular stone in Victorian England as a symbol of clarity and vision, and the true citrine (as opposed to a heated smoky quartz, which is often mistaken for citrine as it has a similar colour) was prized in 1920s' and 1930s' art deco jewellery.

Qualities Often known as the 'merchant's stone' when carried or worn, the citrine can be beneficial in all commercial and business dealings, because it's a stone that attracts financial opportunity and abundance. It is also a crystal of joy, optimism and enlightenment, while enhancing all forms of interaction, negotiation and persuasion.

Abracadabra Hold a piece of citrine in your hand for five minutes while you visualise a future desire, and you will soon see your wish come true.

CANCER

21 June–22 July
Crystal: moonstone
Symbol: the crab
Element: water
Colour: opaque white/soft blue tinge
Keywords: calm creativity, insight, intuition,
    fertile thoughts and feelings

Legend In Roman times the moonstone was worn by travellers as a stone of protection, and was associated with the moon goddess, Diana. It was believed that the goddess was embodied in the stone itself and would guard the wearer against the roaming beasts of the dark night with whom she herself romped.

Qualities A crystal that opens your mind to deeper truths, the moonstone also enhances all forms of psychic or intuitive awareness. Wearing the stone helps to banish negative thoughts and instil a sense of peace and calm. The moonstone is often used as a fertility crystal; its association with the lunar cycle also brings inspirational thoughts and creative ideas to fruition.

Abracadabra Bury a moonstone in the garden (or in a potted plant if you don't have a garden) on a night of a full moon and by the following full moon an empowering, creative idea will come to you.

LEO

23 July–22 August
Crystal: tiger's eye
Symbol: the lion
Element: fire
Colour: burnt yellow/orange/umber
Keywords: focus, abundance, opportunity, tenacity

Legend An ancient Persian princess had a necklace made of 25 tiger's eye crystals, and very soon after, 25 warriors fell in love with her. So confused by having to choose among them, she hid the necklace in her boudoir drawer and never wore it again, and one by one the warriors disappeared and she was left lonely forever.

Qualities This is a stone of questing, adventure and *carpe diem*: seizing the day. It promotes a fiery dedication to your goals, whether they are for a new love affair or a career enterprise. It removes illusion and unblocks self-doubt when worn as jewellery. When carried, the tiger's eye brings focus and reveals truths around all your interactions with others.

Abracadabra Placed in the south-east corner of your home, the tiger's eye can bring success and positive outcomes to confused situations.

VIRGO

23 August–22 September
Crystal: peridot
Symbol: the Virgin
Element: earth
Colour: soft green
Keywords: eloquence, discrimination,
    compassion, clarity

Legend Worn by ancient Aryan warriors, or studded on shields or weapons, the peridot was believed to promote courage and deter cowardice. The Renaissance magician Cornelius Agrippa was convinced that if the stone was held up to the sun it would draw in solar power; if it was then placed on the chest, it would cure all respiratory ailments.

Qualities The peridot brings intellectual clarity and the ability to accept the reality of a situation. But its greatest joy when worn is to enhance self-belief, giving you the power to ask for what you truly want. It also promotes abundance and prosperity. Wear peridot on a romantic date and it will protect you from overthinking and enable you to read between the lines.

Abracadabra If you're going for a job interview or want to sell an idea, the evening before, sprinkle dried basil in a circle around a piece of peridot, leave it overnight and in the morning you will be able to present the perfect pitch.

LIBRA

23 September–22 October
Crystal: blue sapphire
Symbol: the scales
Element: air
Colour: palest blue
Keywords: diplomacy, fidelity, judgement, good fortune

Legend Sapphires of all different colours have been known throughout history as the 'wisdom stone'. The ancient Greek high priestesses used the stone to channel messages from the gods, whereas to the Chinese Emperors the sapphire was a symbol of status and power. Buddhist monks believed the blue variety of sapphire brought spiritual enlightenment and that it had been worn by the Buddha himself while he sat meditating beside the Bodhi Tree.

Qualities The palest blue sapphires are amplifiers of judgement and insight, and can be worn to promote powers of astute instinct and awareness when involved in anything from a difficult romantic situation to a diplomatic encounter. Sapphire is also thought to boost your own psychic or intuitive powers when worn or held during meditation.

Abracadabra Placed in a south corner of your home, blue sapphire helps to encourage fame and fortune into your life.

Scorpio

23 October–21 November
Crystal: obsidian
Symbol: the scorpion
Element: water
Colour: black or dark mahogany
Keywords: security, protection, objectivity, authority

Legend Formed from the cooling lava of volcanoes, obsidian to the ancient Greeks was thought to be the stone that burst through the earth as Hades rose from the underworld to snatch the nymph Persephone, daughter of the goddess Demeter, to return with his prize to his dark home. In the medieval period, obsidian was often used by magicians and occultists for scrying (gazing at the stone as if it were a mirror to see into the future) and other divination techniques.

Qualities Obsidian is the perfect stone to block geopathic stress in the home and to counter negativity from other people. As a stone of protection, it bestows self-reliance and positive thinking, and it clears any emotional confusion. Place this power stone on your desk to enhance all forms of financial or creative dealings; wear or carry it on romantic or business meetings to keep you grounded and to ensure success.

Abracadabra In moments of self-doubt or indecision, place the stone in the palm of your hand, hold it tightly for a few minutes, and you'll feel ready and sure of your direction.

SAGITTARIUS

22 November–21 December
Crystal: turquoise
Symbol: the archer
Element: fire
Colour: shades of turquoise blue and
   turquoise green
Keywords: exploration, travel,
   spontaneity, promotion

Legend Considered a sacred stone by Native American shamans, turquoise was used to call upon the gods and worn as a protective stone during their long nomadic travels across the plains. In ancient Eastern mythology, turquoise was believed to be the Hindu love goddess, Rati's, teardrops.

Qualities Turquoise bestows its wearer with good luck and is thought to be the most important protection stone to carry when travelling. When carried or worn as jewellery, the crystal enhances all new romantic encounters and boosts creative talents.

Abracadabra Place a turquoise in the north corner of your home to activate all career desires and opportunities.

CAPRICORN

22 December–19 January
Crystal: garnet
Symbol: the goat
Element: earth
Colour: dark red, with brownish to purplish hues
Keywords: uplifting, confidence, protective, activates desire

Legend In Eastern mythical traditions, garnets were believed to be dragons' eyes, and were often studded into weapons and shields to give the warrior dragon power. Also known as a carbuncle stone, it was thought by the ancient Greeks that if the garnet was worn as a necklace the wearer would be able to see in the dark, such was the power of its inner light.

Qualities When worn or carried as an amulet when travelling, garnet protects and uplifts the spirit. Whether you require calmness or excitement, romantic highlights or simple friendship, wearing garnet enhances your desire or mood. Lucky for love, business and relationships, garnet is one of those all-round talismanic crystals that brings you all that you truly desire.

Abracadabra Garnet is superb to restore or enhance your libido. Lie face down and place a garnet at the base of your spine (or your partner's) to activate the base chakra (read about the chakras in Chapter 2). Leave for 5 minutes while you feel the 'warmth' of the stone working its magic!

AQUARIUS

20 January–18 February
Crystal: amber
Symbol: the water bearer
Element: air
Colour: amber, shades of yellow, brown, orange
Keywords: purification, balance, wisdom, insight

Legend Although amber is not technically a crystal but fossilised tree resin, it was regarded as a sacred stone by the ancient Greeks. According to one story, Zeus hurled a thunderbolt at the boisterous lad Phaethon, because he was tearing around in his sun-god father's chariot and destroying all the light in the world. When the flaming chariot fell to earth and Phaethon was killed, his mother, Clymene's, tears turned to amber.

Qualities Amber is a great purifying stone. It absorbs negative energy and then dispels it, soaking up bad emotions and negative thinking, and promoting rational thoughts and deeper wisdom. Bringing harmony, clarity and insight to the wearer, it is also believed to lighten the mind, declutter the heart and revive self-belief.

Abracadabra Wear amber on an important date to give you confidence and pure-attraction factor.

PISCES

19 February–20 March
Crystal: amethyst
Symbol: the fish
Element: water
Colour: shades of light violet to deep purple
Keywords: creativity, spiritual insight,
    passion, intuition

Legend Amethyst was revered by the ancient Egyptians as a stone of divine love, and, when worn, would banish all evil. The Romans studded their goblets with amethysts, which were believed to detoxify wine. Indigenous African shamans believed that placing amethyst in an oasis would invoke the storm gods to fill the land with rain.

Qualities Amethyst is not only the perfect stone for stirring the imagination, passions and creating harmony in the home, but also when worn it increases wise thinking, refines thoughts and inspires ideas. It is a great stone for manifesting realistic dreams, forming passionate bonds and promoting all business dealings.

Abracadabra A crystal placed near to the front entrance of your home will ensure that all who pass by will bring positive energy into your world.

Common plants and herbs for healing

Here are the best plants, herbs or oils to include in your spell work. You will find that many of the herbs and oils are used in spells and enchantments together with candles, deities or other symbolic associations. The combination of herbs with your other ingredients will enhance beneficial influences to make magic work for you. Experiment with the different associations, or combinations, of crystals, herbs and other ingredients to create your own spells for specific desires.

Lavender (dried flowers, essential oil or whole plant) Best known for its ability to help people sleep when placed under a pillow, lavender is also used to purify the mind and as an aid to inner and outer beauty, as well as an enhancer of love and happiness.

Rosemary (dried, fresh leaves, essential oil) Essential oil from this common kitchen herb is used for reducing anxiety and clearing brain fog. It enhances mental clarity, relieves stress and aids healing and protection. Sprinkle a circle of oil around any crystal used in a spell or ritual to protect and maximise the crystal's charm and to give you insight into your true intentions.

Basil (dried, fresh leaves, oil) Used mostly in cooking for its incredible flavour, basil was known throughout medieval Europe as the herb of protection and good luck. Hung over doorways at feasts, it calmed all who entered, and it also acted like a well-tailored bouncer to turn away unwelcome guests (in those days, these included demons and spirits too!). Use with money, love and protection spells to boost your good luck and protect you from unwanted intruders or manipulative tacticians.

Thyme (dried, fresh leaves, oil) Another great culinary herb, thyme is used in healing for protection, cleansing and even to encourage abundance and money. When a fresh sprig is placed beneath your pillow, it will help you to have a restful sleep. When you carry or wear fresh thyme, it promotes psychic awareness and makes you irresistible. It can even attract fairies (yes, those invisible little helpmates) to protect your home.

Rose (petals, rose water, oil) Associated with Greek love gods such as Aphrodite and Eros, rose petals and oil are an invaluable tool in love spells. Essential rose oil can help calm the mind, and enhance compassion and unconditional love. Sprinkle rose petals around your boudoir to enhance all aspects of love-making; place rose hips in a shallow wooden bowl to keep your home harmonious and positive.

Sandalwood (oil and incense) This fragrant, aromatic wood is best known when used as incense to cleanse and purify the home. Relaxing the mind, restoring the spirit and increasing your psychic powers, sandalwood enhances all aspects of magic work, and when burnt as incense, is a fabulous aphrodisiac. It is one of the more costly aromatics.

Cinnamon (incense, bark and powder) The beautiful fragrance of cinnamon is usually found in culinary recipes. The tree from which the bark, leaves and berries are produced grows in the spice regions of India, Sri Lanka and parts of Central and South America. Cinnamon incense can be burnt to harmonise the energy of the home and enhance spiritual calm. Often combined with sandalwood to deepen your insight and improve psychic skills, it also attracts romance to you when sprinkled in your shoes or handbag.

Cedar wood (oil) Associated with solar energy and the zodiac sign Leo, cedar can be used in spells to attract success and enhance inspiration. It is also a great protective wood when a piece is placed above the doorway to your home or office. A tiny amount of essential oil dabbed onto the back of your hand helps you to focus on your true goals.

Jasmine (oil or fresh petals) Jasmine's heady, sensual fragrance is used in many spells to draw and attract love to you. The petals can be sprinkled in your boudoir or under your pillow to enhance love-making, whereas wearing jasmine perfume or essential oil will attract attention from those who will see not only your outer radiance but sense the true beauty within you.

Ginger (fresh or dried) A powerful, fiery spice used in many dishes and known for its health benefits, ginger is the spice that attracts money, luck and inner motivation to create outer success. It can also be used in spells to promote fast results or to create passion in a new relationship.

Ylang ylang (perfume or oil) This is one of those flowers that ignites pure lust in the opposite sex. Wear this as a perfume or oil if you're up for a night of passion or a sexy date, when you'll be totally bewitching and irresistible. Ylang ylang can also be worn if you're trying to impress someone in a career change or business deal as it also has an effect of harmonising the balance of yin/yang energy in the environment.

From the heady heights of sensuous oils and herbs, let's now look at the empowering energy of the heavenly bodies themselves: the planets, moon and sun.

The moon, sun and planets

In magic, everything is One. The magical web is made up of an invisible electromagnetic force, which weaves through the colour spectrum, the aura, chakras, mind, body and soul, plants or divination tools. In fact, this universal energy permeates all, so it's understandable that the ancients believed in the power of the stars and planets, and the gods who ruled them. These days, quantum physics also promotes the same idea that 'all is one', and that the heavens and all that is out there are as much a part of us as we are part of them. Drawing down the power of heavenly bodies promotes and amplifies everything else you use for magic. Of course, they can be used as stand-alone icons or symbols to empower you, too.

The moon

The moon and its cycle has been one of the most important heavenly bodies to be used in magic throughout history. The earth's tides, the growing of crops, the lives of creatures, flora and fauna, our body rhythms, and even our moods, are all in some way dependent on the lunar cycle. Be aware of the moon's cycle throughout the days of every week, and use its power when casting spells or doing healing work.

The moon is associated with all things feminine and is represented by the ancient Greek moon goddess, Selene.

In practical magic, we use not only associated symbols but the actual changing energy of the different phases of the moon, whether for dream work, domestic issues, psychic work, emotional and spiritual healing, or protection and beauty.

The moon has four lunar cycles:

New moon This is usually known as the dark of the moon. You won't be able to see the moon for a few days while it is hidden from view. This is considered a secret time, and a time for seeding, preparing and plotting new ideas or spells, which are then ready to be activated with the crescent moon.

Waxing or crescent moon This is the period of growth and beginnings, and it occurs between the first glimmer of a crescent moon and the complete fullness of the full moon. The moon when waxing appears as a right-sided crescent of light, growing bigger until it becomes a full white orb. This is the perfect time to cast all spells to attract, create, inspire, start new projects and seduce.

Full moon The light of the full moon (the sun's light falling directly on the full orb of the moon) creates the most magical time, as it is now complete in combining lunar and solar energy. Use the light of the full moon for spells and enchantments concerning prosperity, knowledge, love, divination and healing.

Waning moon When the fullness of the moon starts to diminish as a crescent moon of light on its left side, this is when the moon is waning towards the dark phase of the new moon. This is the best time to perform spells to do with banishing, releasing, diminishing, letting go and moving on.

The sun

Although the sun is the most important heavenly body in the sky – because life on earth depends on it – we must be a little careful when using its potent energy. Solar power can instil purely self-centred goals (as opposed to using magic for the good of the whole) by even the most sincere and gentle white witch! Of course, without the sun, or our egos, we wouldn't exist, so if you're going to honour anything up there in the heavens, the sun is number one on your list. Remember, however, that it's the centre of everyone's solar system, not just yours.

The sun has always been associated with masculine, potent energy. It represents fire, action, impulse and pride. The energy is hot and dramatic, and using the solar symbol in any magic work may fast-forward events and promote a quick conclusion.

Harness the qualities and symbols related to the sun for achievement, ambition, career goals, leadership, success, action and property negotiations.

Mercury

The closest planet to the sun, Mercury is only a little bigger than our moon. It whizzes quickly around the sun (and takes about a year, like the sun, to get around the zodiac), and its surface can be intensely hot, or intensely cold, because its elliptical orbit means it can be very close or very far from the sun. It was named after the fleet-footed Roman god, Mercury. In astrology and other occult arts, this planet has long been associated with communication, trade, negotiations, tricksters, shape-shifting and short-distance travel.

Work with the symbols and related qualities of Mercury for positive communication, new knowledge, better understanding, travel plans, business negotiations and making decisions. (See page 208 for information on Mercury retrograde as this is a period which can stall our plans, create delays and provoke breakdowns in communication.)

Venus

In astronomical circles, the planet Venus is renowned for its volatile, sulphuric, hell-like atmosphere. In fact, it seems to have little in common with the archetypal image of the goddess Venus after whom the planet was named; however, because it was known by the ancients as both the evening and the morning star, due to its brightness and beauty in the sky, Venus promotes all the qualities of love, passion, desire and physical happiness when used in magic.

Invoke the symbols and qualities associated with Venus for beauty and love spells, sexual desire, getting what you want, self-empowerment and self-esteem.

Mars

The red planet, Mars, might look hot and fiery, due to the red soil on its surface, but this is a cold, inhospitable place. Mars, named after the Roman god of war, has two moons: Phobos (fear) and Deimos (panic), named after the horses that pulled the god's chariot. Mars is associated with courage, fearlessness, action and impulse. This planet enhances drive, motivation and enterprise.

The symbolic energy and powers of Mars are harnessed for success spells, motivation, business opportunities and dealing with challenging circumstances.

Jupiter

With over 50 moons, the giant of a planet, Jupiter, is considered almost a mini solar system in itself. The Roman god Jupiter (the Greek god Zeus's equivalent), was thought to be the most powerful of the gods, who ruled the sky, thunder, and even the Romans themselves! Jupiter is associated with joviality, supremacy, justice and philosophy.

Work with the symbols and qualities of Jupiter's kingly powers to enhance all spells concerned with career changes or business propositions, financial affairs, justice, wealth and discovering the truth.

Saturn

The ancient Assyrians described Saturn as 'a mere sparkle in the night sky', due to it often being only just visible to the naked eye. Named after the Roman god of agriculture and grain, Saturn is associated with protective masculine energy, as well as self-discipline, caution, duty and order.

Channel the symbols and related qualities of Saturn's protective influence in spells to protect business or home, as well as for property dealings, self-reliance, patience and future planning.

Uranus

Invisible to the ancients, Uranus is, however, named after the Greek god of the heavens, Ouranus. The planet is associated these days with collective issues and individual acceptance of change, reformation of ideas and creative or abstract thinking.

Work with the symbolic qualities of Uranus's unpredictable influence in spells where you need to be inventive, to open up to radical ideas or to promote a revolutionary approach.

Neptune

Named after the Roman god of the oceans, the planet Neptune is associated with dreams, fantasy, ideals, seduction, art and music. As the more recently elected ruler of the zodiac sign Pisces, Neptune can be used in all spell work to enhance psychic powers and spiritual healing.

Harness the symbolic energy of Neptune's seductive power to bewitch and persuade others to your way of thinking, or to attract mentors and contacts to you.

Pluto

The small planet Pluto has in recent years been classed as a planetoid by the astronomical community, because it does not fully fit the definition of a planet. It has a strange elliptical orbit, which at times passes closer to the earth than Neptune. Pluto remains important, however, for its magical influence in creating order, and to enhance transformation and unity.

Pluto is an outsider and its symbolic qualities and energies are best used in spells to transform negative thinking into positive results.

The seasons, cycles and festivities

Festivities are held throughout the world to celebrate gods, saints, events, the changing weather or seasons. This ancient human desire to celebrate a particular day or seasonal shift is an expression of both our joy and our acknowledgement of powers greater than our own.

Perhaps, instead of labelling these celebrations as the worship of an actual deity, a myth or a date, we could refer to them as celebrations of an upheld belief that permeates all cultures: the power of the universe. Performing magic on these specific days can help you to stamp the quality of that day upon your spell, adding an extra texture to the enchantment, rather like adding an extra layer of icing on a cake. The following are some important traditional days for adding positive emphasis to your magic healing work.

The solstices and the equinoxes

The solstices are the two days in a year when the sun is either at the highest point in the sky (the summer solstice) or the lowest point in the sky (the winter solstice), and they mark two turning points. The summer solstice (midsummer) in the northern hemisphere is on 21 June when the sun enters the zodiac sign of Cancer, and the winter solstice (midwinter) is on 20 December when the sun enters Capricorn. In the southern hemisphere it's the opposite: midsummer is 20 December; midwinter is 21 June.

The day of the **summer solstice** is favourable for spells to enhance romance, marriage, bonds, creativity, children, new projects, success and goals.

The day of the **winter solstice** is favourable for spells concerned with introspection, understanding oneself, reviewing ideas, revising plans and rejecting outmoded beliefs – in fact, any activity beginning with re-.

The equinoxes are like the waning and waxing moon. The **spring equinox** (when the sun moves into the first sign of the zodiac, Aries) marks the first day of the astrological year and is likened to the waxing moon. Use the spring equinox for fresh ideas, beginning any project and seeing the benefits of the future.

The **autumn equinox** (when the sun moves into the zodiac sign of Libra to mark the second half of the astrological year) is likened to the waning moon. Use the autumn equinox for spells to let go of emotional baggage, to free yourself from ties, take a break from routine and be more spiritually aware.

Deities

As you have seen, the planets are all named after deities. The following gods and goddesses are associated with various aspects of life, and can be invoked or called upon as symbolic or archetypal manifestations to help us in healing magic or to achieve our specific goals.

Below is a selection of Greek deities, whose symbolic power and related qualities I prefer to work with. Depending on your own cultural preferences, you can choose any worldwide pantheon you feel suits you, or you feel an affinity with. If you don't feel drawn to my Greek friends, do a little research on other pantheons such as Celtic, Chinese, Egyptian or Hindu, and see which you feel most at home with. You will find a range of spells and enchantments in Chapter 3, which harness the power of some of these deities.

Selene – the moon goddess Selene helps with fertility, creativity, emotional healing, overcoming fears, self-empowerment, boosting compassion, intuition and psychic power.

Athene – goddess of wisdom This strong-minded lover of truth, Athene can enhance intellectual pursuits, legal affairs, personal protection, strength, business deals and peace.

Demeter – goddess of agriculture Calling on Demeter will align you to spells and magic connected to fertility, motherhood, abundance, reaping rewards and harvesting truth.

Apollo – god of light Apollo's fiery yet illuminating energy is used for spells to help see the light, revealing truth, for inspiration and for divining the future.

Aphrodite – the goddess of love and beauty Call on this goddess for all enchantments and spells to do with love affairs, new romance, beauty, self-belief, attracting others and marriage.

Ares – the god of war and valour He may have been a bit of a brute, but Ares gets things done, and is a brilliant aid for self-esteem, courage, competition, enterprising goals, confidence and asserting oneself.

Hermes – the god of trade, waysides, tricks and ruses Although Hermes was a bit of a trickster, he is the perfect guide in all healing and spell work to discover beneficial travel, trade, good communication, trust, knowledge, insight, logic and reason.

Zeus – the sky god Promiscuous Zeus can help you seduce others with your ideas, or just your personal powers. He's great to call on to help with long-term travel plans, sexual chemistry, adventure and exploration, decision-making, enterprise and initiative.

Kronos – god of time This is a god who might seem austere and cool, but he's the perfect sidekick to help you with business deals, material goals, manifesting dreams, long-term commitment, strengthening ties, protection at home and work, and abundance.

Ouranus – god of the heavens This king of the gods was castrated by his son, Kronos (who schemed with his mother, Gaia, to put an end to his father breeding too many unwelcome siblings). Ouranus' genitalia fell to the sea where they spawned the lovely Aphrodite. Use his magical power to accept change, promote oneself, instigate unconventional ideas, or for inspiration, new friendships and an ideal lifestyle.

Poseidon – god of the oceans Stirring the oceans with his trident, causing tidal waves and shipwrecks, Poseidon isn't a soppy water god; rather, he enables you to ride the waves, go with the flow and take a chance on surfing life instead of wallowing in it. His power, therefore, helps with creativity, boosting talents in music and art, as well as overcoming addiction and believing that dreams will come true.

Hades – the god of hidden wealth Lastly, the god of the underworld was also the god of the hidden treasures of the earth, such as our favourite crystals! Use Hades' power to improve or resolve financial matters, reveal secrets or to get to the heart of an emotional matter, or for transformation and regeneration.

From the world of the power of the gods and goddesses, let's now see how magical energy radiates through each and every one of us too, and how we can draw on that energy to empower ourselves.

Chapter 2

Auras and Chakras – the Magic Within Ourselves

As we've seen, ancient Eastern traditions believe that an invisible universal energy, often known as ch'i (or qi) or prana, flows not only around us but through everything, including rocks, crystals, water, animals, birds, the cosmos and the human body. This energy, when it exudes from the physical body, is known as the aura.

The aura will be coloured by the qualities of our current individual mind, body or spiritual state. The aura is like a web, with shoots of concentrated energy known as the chakras, which form invisible channels through which the universal energy flows, both inwards and outwards. The chakras are like the swing doors of your auric life-force opening up to, and closing behind, this energy flow.

What is the human aura?

Is the aura a cloud-like or misty substance? No, it is an invisible electromagnetic force.

To get a little more technical, in the scientific world of quantum physics, everything in the universe is made up of energy vibrations. These vibrations, or waves, make up the electromagnetic spectrum, which includes sound waves, infrared and ultraviolet radiation, X-rays, gamma rays and light. Waves are measured in wavelength frequency; for example, the distance between the crest of each wave is the *wavelength*, and the number of waves per second is the *frequency*. The longer the wavelength, the lower the frequency. The aura's electromagnetic waves are believed to consist of light, but they are not usually visible to the human eye.

Aura basics

- The aura is made up of electromagnetic particles that radiate from the body.
- The word 'aura' comes from the Greek word meaning 'breeze' or 'air'.
- The aurora borealis, also known as the Northern Lights, is a display of luminous-coloured lights affected by meteorological conditions.

- Modern techniques, such as aura-imaging and Kirlian photography, reveal the state of the aura through the colour spectrum invisible to the human eye.
- We often unconsciously react in either positive or negative ways to someone else's aura depending on the state of their aura and our own.
- Auras are part of the invisible cosmic life-force.
- Many planets have visible auras around them, such as the rings of Saturn or the gas clouds of Jupiter.
- The moon is often said to be haloed, and auras have been likened to halos.
- Halos in art are usually associated with religious or spiritual figures, such as saints, the Buddha, Indian gods and the Virgin Mary.

How to sense other people's auras

Sometimes our auras are out of balance, depending on our inner state of mind, body or spirit, and that's when people who can really 'see' auras will say, 'Your aura looks incredibly blue', or 'It's so red!' Most people, however, will say things like, 'Oh, he's gone red in the face with embarrassment', or 'She's turned green with envy!', so you can see that colour is highly symbolic of our state of being.

To literally see someone's aura is a tricky thing, however, and there's not enough space in this book to explain the many ways to learn to do this. But what you can do is learn to sense your own chakras and auric field, and that way you will begin to experience the presence of other people's auras too. This is a bit like reading other people's body language. Once you start to practise this, you'll find it won't take long for you to understand how colour, character and energy are all interconnected: one is an expression of the others.

Here are two easy exercises to start to learn to sense the aura through touch.

Exercise: touch and feeling

1. Put a fruit, crystal, or even a leaf, in the palm of your hand. (Each has its own unique auric energy field.)
2. Sit quietly, close your eyes and be aware of the object in your hand. Gently close your hand around it to feel it with your fingers too.
3. Now concentrate on what it feels like. What sensations do you get? Prickly (a dry leaf), damp (the fruit perhaps) or hard and potent (a crystal)? You may need to do this for at least 30 seconds before you get any feedback, depending on the state of your own aura.
4. Then, link your response to how it makes you feel: content, restless, happy, confused, amused, sad, worried? This, of course, depends on your own mood, but experiment with as many items as you can to get a feel for different levels of aura energy.

Exercise: sensing qualities

Do this exercise with a friend.

1. Stand face to face with arms extended and palms almost, but not quite, touching.

2. Close your eyes and both concentrate on giving out and receiving energy. Obviously, you won't be able to do this for more than a couple of minutes at a time, or your arms will get tired. Try to experience what the other person's aura is giving out. Is it warm, cold, soft, calm, vibrant or rough, for example?

3. When you give out energy, imagine it flowing from the hara (the key energy centre just below the navel), radiating through your body, and the force passing out through your hands.

4. Take turns to be receiver and giver. Try to sense the quality your partner is radiating – you can use the list of qualities below to give you some ideas:

Calm	Rough
Cool	Sexy
Divine	Sizzling
Dull	Soft
Emotionless	Soulful
Enlightening	Still
Exciting	Vibrant
Genuine	Warm
Hard	Wise

You will eventually be able to feel the invisible aura energy flowing between you and your partner. By sensing the other person's aura, you will also begin to understand their current state of being.

Aura colours

It is rare to see our own aura, let alone another person's, unless we have trained our psychic sense to see them or we have exceptional powers of the mind. Nowadays, there are new techniques that are believed to capture the aura on camera. The pioneering work on aura imaging is still underway by American inventor Guy Coggins, which reveals the aura as a moving field of colourful lights around the body. It suggests that the seven colours of the light spectrum (what we know as a rainbow) make up the essential part of the auric field (plus many other hues in between) and thus through this we can relate these colours to our moods.

By association, we can then relate what we might need to incorporate in our life, or what we might need to change in our life, depending on the state of our aura colours. Auras change with our moods, feelings or experiences. Some people's auras are multi-coloured, whereas others display only one dominant colour.

An expression of our personality

Is colour in the aura the expression of character? If we believe in the interconnection of all things – as we say in magic circles 'as above so below' – this implies that colours correspond to our personality: a zodiac sign corresponds to a crystal, as does a herbal remedy to balancing the chakras. Basically, it is our own current state of being, or personal magic, that colours the pure energy of the universe radiating through our being. These colours are like a personality barcode, revealing specific traits and qualities of ourselves at any one moment in time.

Auras and affinity

Most of us at some time or another describe people in the following ways: 'He just radiates sex appeal', or 'Isn't she glowing with pride?', or 'He's oozing success', and so on. In fact, what we are really describing is someone's aura. This is because although we may not be able to see the colours or feel the energy radiating from someone's body, when we first meet them, this is your unconscious recognition of their aura and the sense of how similar or how different it is to your own. This life force is emitted from every living thing and is coloured by all aspects of your mind, body and spirit – what you think, experience or feel in life.

Instant affinity
When we are attracted to someone, whether sexually, physically, romantically or just because we sense we have something in common with them, our auras are either in complete harmony – colour match or complementary – or they clash to such an extent that we desire the very colour

that is currently diminished in our own aura and want some of theirs to rub off on us! In a way, we are living, walking paintings, with (albeit invisible to the naked eye) colour radiating all around us, so when that perfect person sits down next to us in the bar, or we spot them across a crowded room, we feel an instant attraction to them. We resonate in a positive way to their persona, which exudes through their aura; for example, someone who is radiating, let's say, an aura like an old-master painting – dark, sombre green or umber colours – might find it hard to get on with someone who is radiating an aura like abstract modern art – such as vibrant reds and yellows.

When we meet someone and feel close to them, it's probably because we have similar auras. If we feel miles apart, in contrast, we are challenged perhaps by opposing colours, or we just don't recognise that energy within ourselves. The colour that person radiates may be a colour we are lacking or a part of our personality we are suppressing or not living out. We might just not vibrate to the same colour that that person is exuding at that moment in time. But when we feel an instant affinity with someone, it's usually because we are in the same colour spectrum as they are at that time.

Aura colours and mood

Run through this checklist of ten basic colours and decide which words connect most appropriately to your feelings and mood right now:

Red – fiery, dramatic, inspirational, challenging
Orange – friendly, playful, impressive, optimistic
Yellow – cheeky, adaptable, jovial, chatty
Pink – romantic, kind, harmonious, gentle
Aquamarine – motivated, organised,
    freedom-loving
Green – calm, unflappable, down-to-
    earth, confident
Blue – sensitive, serene, cool, calm
Turquoise – idealistic, peace-loving, laid-back,
    adventurous
Violet – imaginative, shy, dreamy, escapist
White/crystal clear – empowered, self-
    reliant, ambitious

As an example, you might feel in a rather jovial mood, so it's likely your aura is mainly yellow. But if you also chose the word 'ambitious' (white), decide which colour is likely to express itself as a dominant colour. In other words, if you had to choose between 'jolly' and 'ambitious', which one sings louder than the other?

What is your aura signalling?

Remember that the aura changes as you and your circumstances change, and so you will often radiate a combination of aura colours at any one time. But the one that other people and potential love partners pick up on, or are usually attracted to, is your dominant colour.

Even if the described love style is contrary to your true values, it's fascinating to see what other people perceive you to be, as they unconsciously connect to the dominant aura colour.

Decide which quality you feel is most like you and currently dominant, and then turn to the following pages to see what your current love colour is signalling to other people!

Your current love aura

Red Physical fun and sexy adventure are important to you right now, and you're radiating an aura of theatrical spontaneity and fiery passion. You have loads of energy and you need a partner who can keep up with your high-powered sex drive and demanding desires. Flashy and seductive, you appear to bewitch all kinds of potential lovers to your side. When you're out and about, you're the best-dressed or most glamorous woman around. Rivals may be envious of the way you attract people to you like a magnet but being centre stage is the perfect way to catch a lover and keep them hooked.

Orange You're radiating the energy of someone who's spontaneous but not dependent on anyone else for their happiness. Currently, you need a load of space and freedom if a relationship is to work. Inspired by romantic intrigue, you appear extrovert and ready to leap in at the deep end and enjoy yourself. Your optimistic nature is fine, but it could draw the wrong kind of attention to you, unless of course you're up for a fling!

Yellow Currently, you appear to prefer intellectual or intimate conversation to sexual gymnastics. When out and about, you come across as flirtatious and light-hearted, and your sharp, witty mind will keep others entertained and amused for hours. Pals might see you as a threat to their own relationships, because of your quirky, playful approach to seduction. But you're looking for a magical, witty lover of the mind to call your own. You'd never break up anyone else's light romance – or would you?

Pink The ultimate romantic, you exude an aura of a fairytale princess who's about to try on the silver slipper, knowing it will fit only her. No ugly sisters for you; you surround yourself with beautiful companions and like to show off your own physical attributes. Currently, you just want to be in love with love, and you're capable of getting infatuated with more than one potential person. Potential admirers will see you as tender, seductive and loveable, but you can be a little too idealistic about relationships, especially if pink has really taken over your whole being.

Aquamarine You're radiating the aura of an outrageous, independent spirit who doesn't want commitment and is happiest when you're in an unconditional relationship. Getting bogged down in emotions isn't for you, and you have a spontaneous or unconventional approach to love-making. Fun, good humour and intellectual stimulation is more important to you than physical game-playing. Your seductive power is compelling, and you easily attract bold, confident admirers to your side.

Green With a down-to-earth and practical attitude exuding from your aura, you appear ambitious, loyal and committed. In fact, with your sensual aura and seductive grace, you can glide into any room and show you mean pleasure first, business second. Your enthusiasm for love, life and getting things done brings positive energy to others around you. You may not reveal your feelings, but you appear to be the icing on the proverbial cake when it comes to long-term relationships.

Blue Your sensual aura flows out from you like a mountain stream gurgling among twinkling rocks. You appear gentle and shy, yet there's a deep sexual power trickling through those waters. In fact, your aura radiates not only your cool outer persona, but an erotic, magical inner you. You need an intimate, creative relationship, where all is calm and pleasurable. Intuitively you know your best bet is to play an elusive game to attract the right kind of admirer.

Turquoise The unconscious signals you put out when entering a room are of a romantic freedom-lover, who really has no intention of settling down, and just wants a fling, or fun for now. Light-hearted and confident, you appear restless and ready to move on to yet another venue the moment after you've arrived at one. With a twinkle in your eye, and a larger-than-life aura, you seduce quickly, but often don't hang around long enough to discover who you're really with, especially once you've had your way.

Violet You empathise and very quickly identify with whoever you're with, simply because you appear to have no sense of a true identity of your own and have few boundaries. In fact, because you're such a good reflection of the admirers standing before you, they see all their own attributes mirrored in you, and, of course, that makes them feel good to be themselves. This mirroring influence means you're highly attractive, but you also appear dreamy, imaginative, and ready to fall in love with anyone who falls for you.

White/crystal clear You have an air of quiet, sophisticated authority when you walk into a room, so it takes a brave soul to attempt to seduce you. Those drawn to your self-reliant and stunning poise, but with their own sense of achievement, will be welcomed, but it takes you a long time to make any serious commitment to a relationship. Radiating such an independent but serious aura, you might find you attract wealthy or highly ambitious types who see you as a possible power behind their own throne.

The best way to get your aura balanced for holistic health – that is, mental, emotional, physical and spiritual alignment – is to work with your chakras, the gateways to the auric field, which I will now explain.

Chakras

The chakras are localised channels of pure auric energy. The word 'chakra' is a Sanskrit word meaning 'wheel'.

Vibrating at differing frequencies, these vortexes of invisible energy constantly revolve or spiral about and through our bodies in what is thought to be an upward vertical direction. To get a clearer picture of chakras and auras, imagine that a chakra is rather like a shoot sprouting from a stem. The stem is the complete aura. The chakras are individual coloured shoots leading off that stem.

Each chakra is thought to embody one specific colour of the light spectrum: red, orange, yellow, green, blue, indigo, violet. Your aura radiates all kinds of colours and colour combinations dependent on your state or mood, whereas the chakras maintain their own unique colour. Depending on your mood, however, the colour itself might be faded, pallid or washed-out, or it could go to the other extreme: vibrant, strong, gaudy or garish! For example, your dominant aura colour might be green. You are therefore radiating to the world that you're pretty sure you're getting where you want to go in life (and you probably sincerely believe this). In contrast, your heart chakra (green) is a murky pond-water green and reveals that although you may be *radiating* contentment, you are in fact in need of a little self-love and TLC too.

You can't see the chakras, but you can sometimes experience or feel the energy at points around the body; for example, among many of the minor chakras are the hand, feet, elbow and knee chakras. To get a feeling of the power of your chakra energy do this simple exercise with your hand chakras.

Abracadabra Rub the palms of your hands together for about a minute until they are tingling and warm. Separate your hands very slowly and experience the magnetic force between them as they separate. This gives you a sense of the chakra flow of energy around your body.

Exercise: awaken the chakras

Follow this simple exercise to get to know how to sense the energy that flows through the chakras.

1. Sit comfortably on a chair with your back straight and your feet placed together in front of you.
2. Take a few deep, slow breaths and close your eyes.
3. With your fingertips and thumbs touching, and your palms slightly cupped and facing inwards to your body, place your hands about 5cm away from your belly button. This is the aura's centre, known as the hara in Eastern traditions, through which all the chakra wheels revolve and pass. If you continue to hold the position for a minute or so, you will begin to feel a deep warmth radiating into your hands.
4. Now try moving your hands up above the top of your head using the same method. This is the crown chakra, and you will feel a warm sense of well-being generating from this area. The crown chakra is where we are said to be in touch with the higher realms of our spiritual self.
5. Try this method with any of the other chakras whenever you want to awaken and heal that area of your personality according to the descriptions that follow.

How to balance the chakras

To find out if your chakras are out of balance, look at the checklist of chakra statements below to identify which basic statements resonate with your current mood. If there are any to which you feel a strong yes response, the associated chakra will need boosting. See how to do this on the following pages.

- I feel angry about people and things in my life (base chakra)
- I don't have much self-esteem (sacral chakra)
- I'm not as creative or successful as I'd like to be (solar plexus)
- I wish I were more down-to-earth and practical (heart chakra)
- I'm always dreaming of things I will never achieve (third eye chakra)
- I'm depressed and can't snap out of it (crown chakra)
- I am too sensitive and get hurt by what other people say (throat chakra)

If the chakras are not balanced, or if specific energies are blocked, you might find you have negative thoughts or be physically tired or depressed; however, each chakra may need separate reinforcement or need to be subdued, depending on the qualities you feel at the time.

Now, from our box of magic ingredients, we can make

use of the power of crystals. As they vibrate to a similar electromagnetic frequency as the vibrations of the chakras, they can help to reinforce positive energy or bring the chakra back into balance if underactive. (By the way, there are also crystals that can subdue chakra energy if the chakra is overactive.)

Read about each chakra energy below, and if you agree with any of the symptoms of an overactive or an underactive chakra, wear or carry the appropriate crystal. If you find that you agree with more than three different chakra symptoms, obviously don't carry seven stones everywhere you go! Instead, follow the final General Balancing Exercise on page 70.

1. The base or root chakra

Location Base of the spine, centred between the last disc of the spine and the pubic bone to the front. It resonates to the colour red.

Meaning This energy relates to our sense of being grounded. It provides a firm base and a sense of security, plus it controls the basic functioning needs of the body.

Underactive When the base chakra is not energised as it should be, you may be lost in a dream world and not feel in touch with reality. Other people will seem invasive or threatening, and you will be incapable of finishing any project or starting a new one. Red is the colour associated with this chakra, so wear or carry red crystals such as rubies, garnets and red carnelian to enhance your integrity and release you from the fear of others.

Overactive If you have a full-to-brimming base chakra, you'll appear too dominating and pushy, and you might feel angry at the world. To subdue this energy, carry or wear black tourmaline or onyx.

2. The sacral chakra

Location This chakra centre is located approximately a hand's breadth below the navel.

Meaning This is the epicentre of your sex drive, creativity and emotional state. The chakra vibrates to the colour orange.

Underactive You may have low self-esteem about your sexuality and fear getting close to anyone, believing that they see you as a mere sex object. Carry orange carnelian to enhance your emotional confidence and to feel and reach out to others, both sexually and creatively.

Overactive When the sacral chakra is working on overtime, you may be promiscuous or overly demanding. To calm this energy and to be more realistic about your sexual needs, wear or carry jade.

3. The solar plexus chakra

Location Vibrating to the colour yellow, this chakra is situated between the navel and the breastbone and is the centre of our integrity and personal power.

Meaning Solar energy is about ego identity, and this chakra resonates to that sense of willpower, character and strength of ego. We all have an inner sun, and this is where it truly shines.

Underactive If this chakra isn't lit up and vivid in our lives, then we let others dominate us. We might feel afraid of saying what we think, or we worry about what others will think about us. To boost your confidence, wear or carry clear topaz.

Overactive A cocksure polished ego can be to our detriment, too, if we're not aware of the consequences. Then we may become uncaring, self-centred and too proud for our own good. To calm this chakra, wear or carry amber.

4. The heart chakra

Location Behind the breastbone and in front of the spine. The colour green is associated with this chakra and is the energy centre concerned with our feelings of support, closeness and belonging.

Meaning Whether real compassion, unconditional love or spiritual merging, this chakra is also about self-love and giving and receiving love. If we can't love ourselves, we aren't going to find it easy to love another, nor they us.

Underactive When this chakra is feeble, you fear getting hurt and feel vulnerable about deep commitment. Green tourmaline jade or rose quartz restore compassion, self-love and genuine warmth towards others.

Overactive When this chakra is overactive you may be too willing to please or to make sacrifices. Then you either begin to feel a bit of a martyr or you resent your loved ones because you're never doing anything loving towards yourself. To calm this chakra, wear or carry malachite.

5. The throat chakra
Location The throat chakra is found at the lowest end of the throat. The chakra vibrates to the colour blue.

Meaning This chakra acts as the channel for thought, communication, music, speech and writing.

Underactive You might feel shy and prefer to keep your ideas or thoughts to yourself for fear of disapproval. You may misunderstand others or feel you're not as witty or communicative as your friends or contacts. Wear or carry aquamarine to improve your communication skills.

Overactive You think you have all the answers, and never listen to advice. You get angry about other people's stupidity, or their opinions irritate you. To balance, wear or carry turquoise.

6. The third eye
Location Located in the centre of the brow, just above eyebrow level, the third eye vibrates to the colours indigo and violet.

Meaning Often thought to be the centre for our psychic abilities, such as clairvoyance and telepathy, this chakra is also concerned with inspiration and imagination.

Underactive You might refuse to accept the truth or to make it clear what you really want. You may doubt and mistrust all kinds of psychic sense, or muddle your imaginative thoughts with intuitive ones. To get in tune with psychic energy, or to begin to intuitively know what people are really thinking or feeling, carry or wear amethyst.

Overactive You are obsessed with your psychic powers and spend too much time on spiritual or tarot websites. You live with your head in the clouds and don't listen to reason. Wearing malachite will bring you down to earth.

7. The crown chakra
Location Situated literally on the crown of the head, this is the centre for spiritual connection and enlightenment. This chakra vibrates to white, crystal clear and silver colours.

Meaning Awakening the crown chakra allows for the flow of universal wisdom and brings the gift of detachment from fear, and the realisation that all is One.

Underactive You are frustrated by life and love, and there is no joy in the world. You see everything around you as worthless or meaningless. Carry clear quartz crystal to boost this chakra and awaken your spiritual development.

Overactive You think you're the best spiritual advisor in town, or you're an idealist who won't accept the so-called tangible aspects of life. To calm this chakra, wear or carry an opal.

The general balancing exercise

You will need:

    4 pieces of white quartz crystal
    4 white candles

1. To ensure that your chakras are well balanced, take the pieces of white quartz crystal and place them in the north, south, east and west corners of your room.
2. Now, place a candle beside each piece of crystal and then light them in this order: north, east, south, west.
3. Sit in the middle of the room. Either sit cross-legged on the floor with your spine straight, or on a chair with your back supported and your feet equally placed on the floor. Rest your hands gently on your thighs.
4. Face the crystal to the north and the candle flame, then say aloud, or think to yourself the following incantation: 'I am opening myself to the energy of the north to align in harmony with all the other directions so that my chakras will be balanced.' Say, or think, this three times and don't rush. The magic of three is about the harmony of mind, body and spirit.

5. Now do the same with each of the other directions in turn in the order you lit the candles; for example, next you would face east and say: 'I am opening myself to the energy of the east to align in harmony with all the other directions so that my chakras will be balanced.' And so on.

6. Once you have faced all four directions, come back to normal thinking. Take your time, don't rush.

7. Blow out the candles again in the same order as you lit them, take the four crystals and either carry them with you for the rest of the day, or place them beneath your bed overnight to continue powering your chakras with balanced energy.

And finally . . .

The hara

I mentioned that just above the sacral chakra lies what is known as the 'hara'. In most Eastern traditional beliefs, this is thought to be the invisible channel through which universal energy merges with our own physical force field. When we feel balanced and energised, this point helps to balance the chakras, and subsequently our aura radiates harmony and attracts magical power. Keep it in shape and it will bring you the joy you seek.

Exercise: caring for the hara

1. Lie down in a comfortable place, relax and place your hands together – with only your fingers touching, about 5cm below your navel.

2. If you let your hands hover about 2.5cm above this spot of your tummy, you will eventually feel a change of energy.

3. Breathe slowly and deeply. Focus and meditate on this centre of yourself for about three minutes.

4. If you practise this regularly for a few minutes before you go to bed and on waking, you will discover how you can engage in life and love with fewer inhibitions and more tolerance, and how you can enhance your own healing and magical powers into the bargain.

Now let's move on to the practical magic of spells and enchantments in Chapter 3.

Chapter 3

Spells and Enchantments

In the previous two chapters you were introduced to all the magic ingredients you can use to create spells and enchantments. To get you started in your own magical kitchen you will find on the following pages a wide range of spells, rituals and bewitching charms that use many of these ingredients.

Good spell work

Whether you believe in witchcraft, Wicca (a contemporary form of pagan witchcraft) or simply the magic of transforming your life into something better, there are certain, let's say, codes of behaviour when sending spells, wishes, desires or charms out to the universe. The code sums up how to manifest your true desires and cause no harm to anyone else in the process. As the sorcerers of old used to say, 'what goes around, comes around', so if you were intending to send harmful, spiteful or unkind energy in someone's direction, it would be certain to come back at you one day, and threefold, according to most traditions. This is the biggest no-no in modern practical magic, so only do good works for the good of everyone.

The code for good spell work

1. Give out and ask for what you are really happy to receive, and you will be rewarded.
2. Remember that you are doing everything not only for the good of yourself but also for the good of the universe.
3. Never create spells that stop other people from being themselves. The only exception is when you do any protective work to drive away psychic negative energy from others. The spell, charm or placement is not about harming the other person but is intended to block their energy.
4. If you don't believe in the spell working, it won't. Belief is one of the key ingredients of magic. If you believe something is going to happen, you're putting out positive energy to back up your spells. Spells are simply a gathering of associated motifs or symbols to reinforce that belief as many times as is needed to make it clear what you want to manifest. So, don't stop believing once you have cast the spell.

5. When you do achieve your heart's desire, please thank the universe and any deities, symbols or ideas you have called upon for help. Blessings are not difficult to give if you feel blessed yourself.

Spells and charms for love and romance

How fabulous it would be if we could cast a spell and make someone we know fall instantly in love with us? Or perhaps not? You can't force love, you can't hurry it and you don't have power over it, and that means you mustn't try to have power over other specific people either. It's OK to cast a spell to attract an ideal mate but not a specific person.

Here's a range of spells to use for a variety of affairs of the heart.

Bewitching crystals

For every sun sign of the zodiac, there's one crystal that can attract that sun sign person's attention. Again, the intention is not to have power over an individual but to lure certain signs towards you. It won't necessarily make the person fall in love or romance you, but they will 'sniff in the air' the energy to which they feel most comfortable. If you're single, then follow the traditional belief that either 'like attracts like', or, in some books, 'opposites attract'. This means that there are four signs of the zodiac that would complement yours and are worth attracting.

Below are the matches made in heaven, and the challenging but highly sexy ones, as well as the crystals to use to attract a new admirer of that sign.

All you have to do is wear or carry the appropriate crystal to lure your chosen amour and hope to keep them hooked until you can work your own personal magic on them.

The matches made in heaven are:

For Aries – Leo, Sagittarius
For Taurus – Virgo, Capricorn
For Gemini – Libra, Aquarius
For Cancer – Scorpio, Pisces
For Leo – Aries, Sagittarius
For Virgo – Taurus, Capricorn
For Libra – Gemini, Aquarius
For Scorpio – Cancer, Pisces
For Sagittarius – Aries, Leo
For Capricorn – Taurus, Virgo
For Aquarius – Gemini, Libra
For Pisces – Cancer, Scorpio

The sexy challenges are:

Aries/Libra
Taurus/Scorpio
Gemini/Sagittarius
Cancer/Capricorn
Leo/Aquarius
Virgo/Pisces

The crystal you can use to attract each zodiac sun sign are:

Aries – ruby
Taurus – emerald
Gemini – citrine
Cancer – moonstone
Leo – tiger's eye
Virgo – peridot
Libra – blue sapphire
Scorpio – obsidian
Sagittarius – turquoise
Capricorn – garnet
Aquarius – amber
Pisces – amethyst

Love potion number one

If you're going to seduce, be the centre of attention or generally create fine romance in your life, you first need to get in the groove by wearing the number-one love potion. Like any perfect perfume, the magic of mixing different fragrances is an art in itself. Here's a very simple potion you can make at home and will make you the most desirable woman on this planet.

You will need:

3 drops of rose oil
2 drops of jasmine oil
1 drop of sandalwood oil
1 drop of vanilla extract or oil
1 drop of patchouli extract or oil

Mix all the ingredients in a small bottle or container, and leave for one night. Before the next date or assignation when you want to lure someone to you, dab a few drops of the potion behind your ears, between your breasts and behind your knees.

Spell for a new romance

Friday is Venus's or Aphrodite's day, so this is always a good day to cast a spell and ask her to help you find new love or for new romance to come your way. If you perform this spell under a waxing or crescent moon (both of which are positive creative phases of the moon – see page 39), so much the better and the more quickly will you find love.

What you will need:

3 pieces of rose quartz crystal
3 pink tea-light candles
piece of paper
pen
lavender oil

1. Place the three pieces of rose quartz in a horizontal line, with a pink candle behind each one. Light the candles. Sit quietly, and then write down a list of the qualities you are seeking in your romantic partner and a time limit for your search – a maximum of three months is usually thought to work.

2. After you have made your list, write at the bottom: 'Thank you Aphrodite for helping this special person to come into my life.'

3. Sprinkle a few drops of lavender oil onto the paper, and finally write, 'Dear Aphrodite, let he/she be the one for me.'

4. Now wrap the paper around one piece of quartz and bury it in your garden, if you have one. If not, put it in a secret box in a drawer, and leave for three lunar cycles. Let the three candles continue to burn down before removing them. From this day on, get out and about, and the type of partner you seek will soon come to you.

5. At the end of three months, retrieve your crystal from the garden, clean it and cleanse it as described on page 16.

Candle safety

Remember to always place candles into secure holders, or if you are using nightlights, put them on a saucer or in a nightlight holder – and never leave a lighted candle unattended.

How to seduce anyone: Aphrodite's enchantment

Aphrodite was notoriously vain, but also had the power to seduce and attract any god or mortal that took her fancy. Use her power to get your own way, too.

What you will need:

mirror
lipstick

1. First thing on a Friday morning (Aphrodite's day), make sure you look at yourself long and hard in the mirror. You may hate your hair or discover a blemish, but don't let that stop you now. Aphrodite was forever vain and believed she was the fairest of them all. You are now going to *be* Aphrodite, and *be* vain, so you will ooze charisma and will seduce anyone you choose into your arms.

2. OK, look at yourself again. Tell yourself aloud that you're going to be as vain and seductive as Aphrodite all day – and that's that. Write the word 'vanity' on your mirror in lipstick; there's no stopping you now.

3. For the rest of the day, consciously look at yourself in every mirror you pass by. Be so sure of yourself, so vain, so aware of your beauty, so convinced of your power that you see only Aphrodite in you. Each time repeat: 'I am perfect – a beautiful goddess of love and life, and I will seduce [add the name here] into my arms.' Say this over and over again for a whole day to invoke Aphrodite's power. Very soon after, if you truly believe in your charismatic self, the magic will happen.

Charm to see your future lover

This is based on various medieval European folk traditions, which told how young women could see their future husbands.

What you will need:

white candle
silver ring
mirror

small sharp knife
an apple

1. On the night of a full moon, light your candle and place it and the silver ring in front of a mirror. Gaze into the mirror for a few moments to still your mind.

2. Slowly start to peel the apple in one long continuous piece. If it should break, use whichever is the longest piece. Take the apple peel, swirl it around your head three times, then throw it behind you.

3. Take up the ring and say: 'This moon is bound with silver bright to show the name of love tonight.'

4. Turn around, and see what initial the peel has formed (or nearest to a letter shape as possible). This will be the initial of your future lover's first name.

Amber attraction spell

This simple spell can be used to attract a range of strangers to you as you go about your daily chores or business, meanwhile enhancing your own powers of beguilement.

What you will need:

piece of amber
piece of paper
pen

1. During the night of a full moon (only if you can see it in an unclouded sky) gaze up at the moon, looking at it through the piece of amber.

2. As you do so say: 'By all the power of amber true, this moon sends out my love to you.'

3. Focus on the kind of qualities you are looking for in a lover or partner (*not* a specific person) and write down those qualities on the piece of paper. Wrap the paper around the amber, and place it under your pillow while you sleep.

4. In the morning, the amber will be energised, and you can carry it with you or wear it as jewellery. It will act like a magic charm, attracting all those who deserve your love.

Love powder to seduce that first date

When you are about to go on that first, or even a second, date, dust some of this love powder about your body – behind your knees, between your breasts and a little behind your earlobes. Finally, rub some powder through your hands and, when you first touch your date, perhaps in a friendly gesture or just by mistake, they will immediately want to know you better.

What you will need:

a handful of small dried rosebuds
5 dried rose hips or 5 hibiscus seeds
1 small tsp of dried lavender
a pinch of ground cinnamon
a handful of rice flour

1. Grind up all the ingredients, except the rice flour, in a pestle and mortar. (The by-hand approach is more natural than using a grinder, and you are putting all the effort

into making this magic work, but if you don't have time or are not able to get hold of a pestle and mortar, use a coffee grinder.)

2. Mix with the rice flour until it's fairly smooth. Once your powder is made, store it in a airtight container and dust as appropriate before you go on the date.

Instant spark

As with all spells, be careful what you want to attract to you. With this charm you are not only attempting to attract strangers to you, but also hoping that there will be that instant 'spark' that we all seek in a romantic attachment. Of course, many relationships don't begin this way at all, but if you're looking for an instant buzz, this little spell will set you up for mutual infatuation (whether it lasts or not is another spell story).

What you will need:

2 rosebuds
2 peppermint leaves
2 tsp rice flour
the Two of Cups tarot card
2 garnet crystals

1. First make your dry powder. Crush up the rosebuds and peppermint leaves in a pestle and mortar, or a grinder. Add the rice flour, blend and leave for a few hours for their essential natures to merge.

2. Take the Two of Cups tarot card (the card of attraction) and place it face up on a table. Place the two garnets on

the card, one on the image of the woman, and the other on the image of the man.

3. Sprinkle a little of the powder onto the garnets and say: 'With this potion love will spark; with these garnets no more dark.'

4. When you are ready to go out on a blind date, or about to go to some unknown party or new venue, or just to socialise, dust some of the powder onto one of your hands and rub between your fingers. Put the garnets in a pouch and carry them with you. When you meet someone you fancy, touch them with your powdered hand and the magic spark will ignite.

How will we get on?

Here's an easy enchantment to find out if a new relationship will work – or not.

What you will need:

pink candle
piece of pink tourmaline
2 leaves of fresh basil

1. Light the candle and pour a few drops of hot wax onto the crystal.

2. Immediately, take the two leaves of basil and place them on the crystal.

3. Now notice what happens:

- If the basil leaves don't burn or shrivel, the relationship will be harmonious.

- If they sizzle or shrivel up, there will be quarrels.
- If they fall off the crystal, love will burn out quickly.

Abracadabra You can sprinkle basil leaves over your lover's body for complete fidelity!

Magic ring spell for true intention

There are times when each one of us has met someone but just doesn't know where the relationship is going. This spell won't make someone love you if they don't, nor will they commit themselves to you if they can't or won't. What it will do, however, is reveal the truth of your lover's intentions very quickly, when action speaks louder than words.

What you will need:

5 tablespoons of rose water
2 basil leaves
a sprinkle of dried lavender flowers
plain, silver ring
piece of paper
pen

1. Put the rose water, basil and lavender into a large glass. Drop the ring into the glass.
2. Write down on a piece of paper what kind of relationship *you* want from the other person. Choose one of these: short-term exclusive; long-term exclusive; a fling.
3. Put the paper on a window-ledge or outside covered

space during the night of a crescent moon with the glass placed on top.

4. The next day, remove the ring and wear it on a chain around your neck or on your finger, and the truth of your lover's intentions will be revealed by the full moon.

A spell to make sure we keep in contact

When you have finally seduced someone and got to know them well enough to see a future together, there are times when you may be apart and not in constant contact, even in this day and age of texts and mobile phones. To keep the communication channels well and truly open, and for good mutual contact, perform the following spell under a crescent new moon.

What you will need:

pen
2 slips of paper (preferably torn from the same sheet
    and about the same size)
2 red candles
piece of citrine

1 Write your name on one piece of paper, and your beloved's on the other.

2. Place the paper with your name written on it on the table with your name horizontal before you, and your lover's slip of paper placed at right angles across it to make a cross.

3. Light the 2 red candles and put one to the east of the crossed papers and the other to the west.

4. Finally, place the citrine (which is the crystal of

communication) in the middle of the cross. Let the two candles burn down, and leave the crossed papers and the citrine in place until the full moon. You will be assured good communication and dialogue as your relationship flourishes.

A love charm for sexual harmony

We all want love to be a mixture of romantic dalliances, excitement or intrigue and, of course, physical passion. Sometimes our sexual needs may not gel with those of our partner; sometimes we merge in orgasmic bliss. To ensure more harmony and less disappointment in the boudoir, make the following secret aphrodisiac charm.

What you will need:

red wax (see method)
sharp knife
2 needles
a little jasmine oil or perfume
2 red rose petals

1. If you don't have any red wax hanging around in your kitchen – which is very likely – burn down a red candle by letting the wax drip from it while you hold it at an angle over a dish, until there is a large waxy puddle. Leave it to cool and set.
2. Now roughly carve out two hearts from the wax.
3. With one needle scratch your name onto one heart, then set the needle aside next to the heart.
4. Use the other needle to scratch the name of your lover

onto the other heart, then set the needle aside next to the second heart.

5. Drizzle a little jasmine oil, or spray the jasmine perfume, over both hearts, then place your partner's on top of yours (depending on how you like your sex!). Put the two rose petals on top of the wax hearts.

6. Take up the two needles in turn (remembering which is which). As you take up the first needle, say: 'This is the needle to represent the love my partner will show to me.' Now take up the other needle and say: 'This needle is a symbol of the love I will show my partner.'

7. Place the point of your partner's needle through the eye of your needle, then put the needle 'union' on top of the rose petals.

8. Gently place the little love-heart bundle and its accessories somewhere discreet or hidden in your boudoir or bedroom. You can be assured of sexual harmony from now on.

Made-in-heaven magic pouch

Apart from sexual harmony, we also depend on a variety of other affinities to manifest perfectly fine relationships. After all, the orchestra of love is a melange of different needs, desires, wants, workloads, stresses and struggles, isn't it? We worry about the other, the other worries about us, and so on. To maintain a strong bond and a firm belief in one another through thick and thin, and through all the joys as well as the difficulties in love, create this magic pouch to carry with you to reinforce and affirm your relationship.

The number five figures prominently in this spell, simply because using the symbolic five elements in the

Chinese art of harmony, feng shui, is said to create the perfect balance for a relationship made in heaven.

What you will need:

pen
small scrap of paper
5 tiny garnets
5 drops of lavender oil
5 dried sage leaves
5 silver coins
pouch (made of velvet or silk)

1. Write the following five lines on the paper:

> *'This love is pure,*
> *This love is solid,*
> *This love is true,*
> *This love is forever,*
> *This love is mine and yours.'*

2. Put the paper and all the other ingredients into the pouch and put it under your bed for as long as you want this love to last.

A banishing spell for a past love

Of course, we sometimes need to 'remove' ourselves from the past, or forget an ex and move on. Alternatively, we have an ex who might not have detached him or herself from us, and the longer we give others hope, the worse it gets for both people involved. Alternatively, we might still be hanging on to the past, wishing 'if only' or wishing we could get back with someone who has long since moved on themselves. This is where we need to dump our emotional baggage and get out of that hallway of deception!

To enable someone to let go, or for you to move on, this spell will ensure that they, and you, continue to grow and love yourselves, and for both to be able to love someone else in the future. What you will need:

white candle
pen
piece of paper
3 small pieces of obsidian or onyx
1 apple
paper bag

1. First light the candle, and then draw a triangle with the main point to the north on the piece of paper.
2. Place the paper underneath the candle and put the three pieces of obsidian on each of the triangle points.
3. Call on the god of time, Saturn, to assist you by closing your eyes and affirming: 'The time has come and all be well, for soon we'll be no more to tell.'
4. Leave the crystals on the paper until the candle burns right down. One piece of obsidian represents you, another your ex and the third, the past.
5. Take the three pieces and the apple, and put them in a paper bag, then bury it. As you bury the bag, repeat to yourself again the same petition you made to the god Saturn. Very soon, either your ex or yourself – or both of

you – will have learnt to let go and love again. Leave your buried treasure to work its magic for you.

For calming a stressful relationship

Do you get stressed by your partner? Does your partner get stressed because you are? This is a calming spell and will take a couple of months to work, but gradually harmony, peace and relaxed living will return.

What you will need:

a square of paper
pen
a handful of lavender flowers
4 pieces of blue lace agate

1. First, make a magic number square. This is simply a square divided into 9 equal squares, and the numbers placed as shown in the diagram overleaf. (The numbers all add up to 15 when added in rows, across or downwards. Fifteen is a powerful number in magic and feng shui.)
2. Write the letters of your first name on the numbered squares as follows. Let's say your name is Helen and your partner's name is Jeremy. Starting at square number 1 – write the first letter of your name, H, beside 1. Now go to 2 and write E, the second letter, then at square 3, write L, at 4 write E and at 5 write N. If your name has more than those 9 digits, you simply carry on working round by going back to 1 again and adding the appropriate letters. When you have added your name, write your partner's name in the same way starting where you left off, so in

this example, you would have the J of Jeremy at number 6, the M of Jeremy at 1 alongside the H of Helen, and the Y of Jeremy at number 2 alongside the E of Helen.

3. Once you have created your magic square, carefully sprinkle the lavender flowers over it, and thank the goddess Eirene (the Greek goddess of peace) for helping you to bring peace to your relationship.

4. Now place the pieces of agate – one on each corner of the square – and leave for one lunar cycle, preferably starting from a crescent moon. You will gradually find that peace and harmony are restored between you and your partner.

Magic number square

4	9	2
3	5	7
8	1	6

Healing enchantments for well-being and beauty

There is nothing more vitalising than actually wanting to pamper and nurture yourself, or just to make yourself more beautiful than you already are. As you probably know, beauty is not just a superficial thing; it arises from deep within us, from our spiritual or soulful self. That's why some people who may appear unattractive in the conventional sense of what beauty is or isn't, can actually be more beautiful than their external features. We all have an issue or two about how we look: we don't look like specific celebs, we have a wrinkle or a spot, and so on. But most of this self-sabotaging thinking is the result of our biggest psychological demon: a lack of self-esteem.

Now's the time to redress the balance and let your true beauty shine and regain that self-worth. Alternatively, there are spells here to enhance a general sense of well-being, not just for yourself, but also for those around you and in the home.

Beauty charm

This is a general charm for all-round everyday beauty, so that wherever you go your innate beauty will shine through and illuminate your revitalised and radiant aura.

What you will need:

3 acorns (the ancient symbol of eternal youth)
a few strands of your own hair
silver ring
pouch or charm bag

1. During the night of a full moon, take your three acorns, the hair and the silver ring and leave them on a window ledge to be charged with lunar power.
2. The next day, wrap your hair around the acorns and

loop the ends through the silver ring. Place this in a small pouch and carry it with you wherever you go, for constant beauty empowerment.

A holistic potion to protect yourself

Create this wonderful potion to restore your vitality, and also to protect your aura and chakras from outside negative influences. This will leave you free from stress and beautifully confident.

What you will need:

- piece of moonstone
piece of onyx
a few drops of ylang ylang oil
a few drops of patchouli oil
red silk pouch or charm bag

1. Pick up the two crystals using your writing hand, and as you do, say:

> 'With black and white, and night and day,
> This spell will cast all dark away.
> Protect me now, and every day,
> Protect myself to go my way.'

2. Next, drizzle a little oil on both the stones, and place in the silk pouch. As each day goes by, the stones will absorb the oil fragrance and bring you greater and greater all-round protection.

An elixir for spiritual healing

There are times when we don't feel at all in touch with our spiritual or soul-centred side. We may have been too occupied with material life, career or relationships. But there is a time and a place for everything. This enchantment will bring you back to the spiritual or divine side of yourself and put you in touch with the universe.

What you will need:

2 white candles
jasmine petals, oil or perfume
about 50ml rosewater
large spoonful of acacia honey
hand mirror

1. Perform this enchantment on the night of a full moon if possible. Draw a bath. (If you don't have a bath you can replicate this in the shower by combining the ingredients to make a potion, and using it as a shower cleanser.)
2. Light the candles and put them at the end of the bath, or in a safe place where they won't fall over or into your bath.
3. Sprinkle the jasmine and rosewater into the bathwater and stir in the honey. Put your mirror by the bath.
4. Get into the bath, then take the mirror and gaze at yourself as you luxuriate in the water. Imagine all the universe is there in the reflection of yourself in the mirror. See the light shining from you, feel the glow of spiritual connection as you smell the gentle fragrance. In the morning you will feel spiritually revitalised and healed.

Crystal charm for a happy home

Well-being begins with a happy home, so place the following ingredients in a safe place in the home to create a magical, peaceful and creative atmosphere around you.

You will need:

3 pieces of green jade for fortune
3 pieces of tiger's eye for luck
3 pieces of moonstone for spiritual happiness
3 pieces of fire agate for integrity
bag or pouch

Place all 12 pieces of crystal in the bag and leave it in the south-east corner of your home to invoke happiness and well-being for all the family all year round.

Protection spell for house clearing

For general well-being we also need to protect ourselves and our homes from the negative energy of people who step over the threshold, or from the environment and surroundings. (See Chapter 4 on psychic protection for more information.) Weave this spell whenever there is a period of difficulty in your life so that you, your family and friends, and your home are in harmony.

What you will need:

piece of white quartz crystal for each room
of your home
piece of black tourmaline for each room
of your home

sage wand (can be bought in most mind, body and
    spirit shops or online)

Place the crystals in each room of your home, then go to
the main entrance door, light your sage wand and begin to
walk slowly around the home, visiting each room in turn.
Swirl the wand in a clockwise circle around the crystals as
you pass by. Each time you enter another part of the home,
say: 'With this wand I bless and cleanse this home of all
negative energy.' Do this in all parts of the house or home,
and then return to the front or main entrance.

The home is now cleared of negativity, and leaving the
crystals in place for one lunar cycle, preferably from one
new moon to the next, will amplify this protective power.

A charm for pure sensuality

Exuding sensuality is what we do naturally, but there are
times when we don't do it well, or we repress or ignore
our physical glamour at the expense of overthinking or
being bound by our emotional state, or we may just be
having a bad-hair day.

Here's a simple charm to use whenever you want to
enhance your sensual aura and cast an air of glamorous
allure wherever you go.

What you will need:

opal
a handful of orange blossom flowers or rose petals
full-length mirror

1. Place the opal and the flowers in front of the mirror.

2. Now undress – yes, undress. Stand naked before the mirror and, before you even start to nit-pick about boob size, fat, lack of muscle, or whatever your favourite self-reproach trick might be, say aloud:

> 'I am the fairest of them all,
> Beauty and sensual delight am I,
> This trick will lure all to my side,
> And every touch will be so mine.'

3. Now take up the flowers, close your eyes and gently rub them over and around your body – any bits you like – and also the bits you don't like so much. Let them fall to the ground when you have had enough (do this for at least one minute), then open your eyes and see in the mirror the sensual aura you have created. You are now revitalised and ready for action.

4. Take up the opal and hold it for one minute, then thank the universe and the goddess of sensuality herself, Aphrodite, for your renewed sensual power.

5. Get dressed and take the opal with you wherever you go as a symbol of your sensual charm.

Elixir for healing the chakras

Sometimes we feel out of balance, out of sync with others, or just out of sorts. Working with our chakras (as we've seen in Chapter 2) can help to restore harmony to mind, body and spirit/soul. This simple healing magic will soon make you feel at one with the universe again.

What you will need:

blue lace agate (for the throat chakra)
peridot (for the heart chakra)
citrine (for the solar plexus chakra)
amber (for the sacral chakra)
red jasper (for the base chakra)
azurite (for the crown chakra)
amethyst (for the third-eye chakra)

1. Lie down on your back and place the seven stones on the appropriate chakra points (see pages 65–9).
2. Lie still for five minutes while you imagine your chakras opening up like a blossoming flower and allowing all the good energy to enter, and banishing all negativity.
3. Now, gradually imagine each chakra closing down; imagine them closing like shutters or like a flower that closes its petals at night.
4. Gradually come back to normality, remove the stones and keep them in a safe place to replenish you whenever they are needed.

Enchantment for inner beauty

We can sit in lovely baths and douse ourselves in magical flowers and essential oils, but when it comes to beauty being more than skin deep we need a different kind of magic to get that inner light truly shining. This spell is best performed on either the spring equinox or summer solstice, or first thing in the morning, to amplify the power of new beginnings and change.

What you will need:

2 rose quartz crystals
2 pieces of red jasper or ruby
clear white quartz crystal
green jade

1. Place the rose quartz crystals in a south corner of your home, the red jasper in the west, and the white quartz crystal in the east. Place the green jade in the north, and then stand in the centre of your home and call upon the four winds of change, like this:

> *'I call on you the south wind to fill me with*
> *beautiful light,*
> *I call on you the west wind to fill me with*
> *sensual allure,*
> *I call on you the east wind to fill me with delight,*
> *I call on you the north wind to fill me with*
> *inner truth.'*

2. Leave the crystals in place for a day and a night, and you will be revitalised both inside and out.

Charms and talismans for manifesting goals and prosperity

Everyone wants to achieve their goals or to become wealthy – although wealth is about inner richness as well as outer effect. Either way, if you're up for manifesting a dream or to attract abundance, here's a selection of ways to work with that special magic.

Thyme money talisman

Associated with compassion and confidence, thyme was often used to encourage good financial dealings and fair trading.

What you will need:

banknote of any denomination
3 sprigs of thyme leaves
length of twine or thread

1. Take the banknote and fold it around the thyme leaves. Fold it once more to make a little package, then tie it up with the thread.
2. On the night of a full moon, bury the package in the garden or in a pot, and your money and financial know-how will soon flourish. Once you have received monetary contentment, dig up the banknote and spend it!

Abracadabra If carried in a pouch, thyme attracts moneyed contacts, or more customers if placed near the entrance to your business.

For manifesting all-round prosperity

Call on the help of the Roman goddess of good fortune, Fortuna, and this spell will bring positive financial flow and a general sense of wealth in all its forms into your life. Be patient, believe, and you will manifest what you truly desire.

What you will need:

green candle
piece of malachite
banknote
patchouli or cedar incense or oil
gold ring or gold coin

1. Find a suitable shelf, table or ledge where you can leave these items until the candle has burnt right down.
2. Light the candle and place the crystal to the north of it. To the east, place the banknote. To the south place either the lit incense stick in its holder or a few drops of the oil in a small bowl. To the west place the gold ring or gold coins.
3. Now call on Fortuna to help bring you prosperity and good luck in all financial dealings. Say aloud: 'Fortuna bring abundance true; this day I send my trust to you.'
4. Let the candle burn right down before you remove all the items, then put them in a safe place such as a box or a private drawer, and the magic will soon begin.

To achieve a goal

Whatever your goal – a new job, a change of fortune, a success story, finishing that novel, or painting a master-piece – this simple enchantment, with the help of the planet Jupiter, will attract to you all the necessary energy to fulfil your desire.

What you will need:

image of the planet Jupiter
piece of peridot
piece of aventurine
a sprinkling of ground cinnamon
pouch

1. On a Thursday (Jupiter's day) put the image of Jupiter in a special place where you can leave it undisturbed for one lunar cycle.

2. Place the peridot and aventurine in the centre of the image, and then sprinkle the cinnamon over the crystals. Say: 'Bless you Jupiter for helping me to achieve my goal, which is [say exactly what your goal is].'

3. If you haven't achieved your goal after one lunar cycle, repeat the spell, but this time remove the two crystals. Leave the Jupiter image in the same spot, and place the crystals in a pouch. Carry them with you to maximise the same intention.

Wealth enchantment

The best day to perform this spell is on a sunny Sunday when the energy of the sun will be on your side. (If the sun is covered by clouds, you must wait until the first opportunity for sun on a Sunday!) You can either place this in your workplace or in the home, depending on where you truly want your wealth to appear.

You will need:

1 tsp grated nutmeg
1 tsp ground cinnamon
1 tsp ground allspice
4 whole cloves
4 small pieces of jade
small pouch (preferably gold coloured to
    represent wealth)

1. Mix the nutmeg, cinnamon and allspice together. Put all the spices and the jade into the pouch and close it.
2. Take it outside into the sunshine and hold it up to the sun. Repeat the following: 'This pouch is filled with riches fine; and one day soon this will be mine.'
3. Take your pouch and hang it near the front door of your home to bless your home, or hang it in your workplace near your desk to bring you the wealth you seek.

Talisman for prosperity and wealth

Here is another way to attract wealth and happiness to you. In many Eastern or ancient civilisations, rice was thought to be both sacred to the gods and beneficial to our prosperity. This simple talisman will attract all-year-round wealth.

What you will need:

white rice, as needed
cup
3 or 4 small pieces of jade, depending on depth
    of your cup
gold candle

1. Place a layer of rice in the bottom of the cup, then add a piece of jade, then another layer of rice, and so on, until you have reached the rim.

2. Light the candle and place it to the south-east of the cup and let the candle burn down.

3. Transfer the cup of rice to the south-east corner of your home, and leave it for as many months as you want to attract wealth. It's believed that as the rice expands, absorbing the humidity in the atmosphere (very gradually), so too will your wealth grow.

Abundance spell

This spell uses coins. The higher their denomination the better, because, for example, silver coins are worth more than copper ones, and therefore they are symbolic of more abundance. But if you can only spare small copper pennies, or similar, the spell will still work.

What you will need:

white candle
a handful of coins

1. Light the candle and sit quietly for a few moments. Imagine the universe is going to provide you with the abundance you seek. Obviously, if you ask for 'just a little more' you won't get much! Be brave, be brazen, and ask for what you truly desire and say how much out loud!

2. Take the handful of coins and then scatter them either under a cupboard or a bed, or under a thick rug or

carpet — anywhere they won't be seen or disturbed, and where they won't clog up your Hoover or get eaten by the dog. As you scatter them, repeat: 'Scatter money on the floor; watch it come in through the door.'

3. Repeat this chant at least 10 times as you scatter the money around your home. You can scatter the coins in just one place or several, but according to feng shui principles, the best place is a south-east corner of your home. Now wait for the results!

4. When you get an increase or abundance in whatever way you asked for, sincerely thank the universe. You can repeat this spell as often as you like as long as you are always clear about how much you want to receive and remember to thank the universe for its gift.

Talisman for a successful business

Whether you work at home or in an office, this simple talisman will boost your business interests.

What you will need:

piece of black tourmaline
piece of onyx
3 pieces of malachite

1. Either in the room in which you work, or, if you need to be more discreet you can do this on your desk, or in a drawer, place each of the stones in the following positions. First, black tourmaline in the north area of your room, desk or drawer, onyx in the south area, one piece of malachite in the east area, another in the west area, and the

last piece placed in the centre of the room or desk. If you looked at it from a bird's eye view, you would see a perfect cross, with a central stone.

2. Rotate the stones once a month (by moving them on one compass point at a time) to boost their protective power during a waxing phase (between a new moon and a full moon) to bring ongoing success.

Spells and lures for career or life direction

Spell to attract good fortune

We all need some good luck when we set off on a new journey, whether for a change of career or lifestyle. This simple little magic trick will benefit you in all that you desire.

What you will need:

pouch or small purse
small piece of black tourmaline
as many coins as you can cram into the pouch
3 pieces of citrine

1. Fill the pouch with the tourmaline and coins. Place the pouch above or beside the main entrance to your home. Hide it discreetly behind a potted plant or on a high ledge or similar to attract fortunate people to enter the house and to protect you from anyone whose intentions are not in your best interests.

2. Place the citrine pieces in a triangle shape in the drawer of your desk. Now wait for magical good fortune to enter your life.

A lure for positive decision-making

Work magic with a piece of white quartz crystal for positive decision-making.

What you will need:

pen (if needed)
paper (if needed)
white quartz crystal

1. When you need to make a decision, think about the decision you have to make. Is there only one choice – an either/or situation? – or are there many possibilities? If there is more than one choice, write them down as a list.
2. Now take up the piece of white quartz crystal in your writing hand.

If there is only one choice, as you grip the white quartz crystal in your hand, close your eyes and relax for a minute or so; you will feel what is truly right for you to do. This is where your intuition is being enhanced by the power of the crystal.

If there is more than one choice, read each sentence aloud, and feel the energy of the white quartz crystal in your hand. When you feel a strong vibration, you will know that this is the decision to take.

A spell to enhance wisdom and knowledge

Sometimes we just want more knowledge about a subject or business, or to acquire wisdom about our career or pathway direction before we take the risk of setting off. This spell will give you deeper insight into whatever you want to know.

What you will need:

blue candle
a book of your choice
3 pieces of lapis lazuli

1. Preferably perform this spell during the first waxing phase of the moon when the energy is enhanced. First meditate or concentrate on what you want to know. Continue thinking about exactly what it is as you light the blue candle.
2. Open the book and place it in front of the candle.
3. Place the three pieces of lapis lazuli in the shape of a triangle on one page of the book. Keep thinking about your desire for knowledge, and then put both your index fingers pointing into the middle of the triangle.
4. Say: 'By the words of Mercury, I will know more than I already know, I will have deeper wisdom and insight, I will be blessed with truth and revelation about [add whatever it is you truly want to know about].'
5. Remove your fingers, and leave the book and stones while the candle burns down, then remove the stones from the book and your insight will begin.

A charm to promote your reputation

Whether you want to climb the success ladder or you need to ensure that your reputation is impeccable, this spell will promote your integrity and bring you the desired results.

What you will need:

mirror
2 green candles
piece of fire agate
white quartz crystal

1. Perform this spell preferably during the period of a waxing moon for greater success. Prop the mirror against a wall if it's not freestanding.
2. Place the two green candles in front of the mirror, one to the left and one to the right, and light them.
3. Between the candles place the fire agate on the left and the white quartz on the right.
4. Take up the agate in your left hand and hold it for a few seconds as you gaze at yourself in the mirror.
5. Say this enchantment:

> 'For all these deeds be done for me,
> For all success I seek to be,
> My strength it grows from day to day,
> To bring repute in every way.'

6. Next, replace the agate, and take up the white quartz crystal in your right hand and repeat the spell.
7. Finally, take up the agate in your right hand, the white

quartz crystal in your left hand, and hold them up towards the mirror; then repeat the charm one more time.

8. Replace the crystals in their initial places, and say: 'Bless you stones for an accomplished future.' Let the candles burn down before you remove the crystals.

By the pricking of my thumbs – to attract good mentors or contacts

The three witches in Shakespeare's *Macbeth* were well into using newts' entrails, toads and other beasty-type things to do their magic work, but they were also known for that well-known line, 'By the pricking of my thumbs, something wicked this way comes.' The 'pricking' is simply a tingling vibration warning of something unfavourable. The same tingling can tell us if something good is coming our way. Here's how to switch it in your favour.

What you need:

2 orange candles
pin

1. During a waxing moon phase, place the two candles beside one another. Take up one and scratch your name into the candle wax along one side using the pin. On the other candle, scratch the names of anyone you want to help you in your career, whether mentors or contacts. If you don't know them by name, just write, 'mentors' or 'contacts' or both.

2. Now light the two candles, and, as they begin to burn down, say three times, 'By the pricking of my thumbs, someone good will come along.'

3. Let the candles burn right down before you extinguish them.

4. As you go about your daily affairs, rub your fingers and thumbs together each time you enter a building or room, or go into a meeting, if you talk to new contacts on the phone, and so on. Each time you do so, if your thumbs tingle, you know you are about to meet someone with a positive influence.

Job interview charm

The night before an interview or similar, perform this little spell to be inspired by the planet Mercury to bring you the gift of the gab as well as good luck.

What you will need:

> a silver-coloured, or real silver, object, such as a
> ring, bowl, photo frame (anything as long as it is
> silver and reflective)
> mirror
> 2 pieces of tiger's eye
> pouch, purse or bag

1. Place the silver object in front of the mirror. (Both these items represent the reflective aspect of Mercury's power of communication and exchange.)

2. Hold the pieces of tiger's eye, one in each hand, then sit down and close your eyes.

3. Visualise yourself at the interview, and how easy it is to impress. You radiate confidence and experience, or whatever skill you need to bring to the table.

4. Open your eyes and say to yourself in the mirror, 'Thanks to the power of Mercury, I will get the job/close the deal [or whatever it is you're after].'

5. Place the two crystals in front of the mirror overnight.

6. In the morning, take up the crystals and carry them with you in a pouch to enhance all aspects of your interview so that you will achieve positive results.

Make a wish, but be careful what you wish for – enchantment

There are some wishes that can never be fulfilled, because sometimes we have outrageous fantasies of fame and fortune which, by the laws of attraction and averages, are unlikely to happen. But, if you truly wish for something that you know is possible, or attainable, and you know it is not just wishful thinking, perform this spell to help you fulfil your desire.

What you will need:

pen
piece of paper
a spoonful of dried rosemary leaves or flowers
a spoonful of dried thyme leaves or flowers
3 acorns
silk pouch

1. Write a specific wish on a piece of paper and put the paper, herbs and acorns in the pouch.

2. Shake gently, and as you do so, repeat your wish aloud, and ask for the universe to make your wish come true. Soon it will, so be careful what you wish for!

Call on Athene for a successful day

The goddess Athene was wise and courageous. She made it her business to be strong-willed and above reproach. Call on her power whenever you want to make a real success of a project or deed, or you just want a day of achievement

What you will need:

2 green candles
piece of malachite

1. Light the candles and place the crystal between them. Say aloud what you hope to achieve: a particular project or just a successful day. Then say: 'Thank you Athene for your trust and energy.'
2. Next, blow out the candles and take the malachite with you on your travels.
3. Hold the stone in your left hand before you embark on any new deed, and visualise your success. Rub the stone in a clockwise direction with your thumb whenever you want to reinforce or boost your success.

Spell for a new intention

Here is a quick way to get the universe to listen to a new intention – not so much a wish, but simply something you have to do next, which can help to make you a better future. Just make sure you know exactly what it is before writing it down.

What you will need:

pen
piece of paper
white candle
stick of sandalwood incense

1. Write your intention on the piece of paper and place it beside the lit white candle.
2. Light the sandalwood incense, and then place it in a holder to burn.
3. As your sandalwood and candle burn, your intent, or wish, will be transmitted upwards in the vapours to merge with the universe and seal a positive intention. Let both of them burn out naturally and your intention will manifest.

A charm for a positive lifestyle change

We all arrive at the odd crossroads in life where we have to make choices and believe that a better lifestyle lies down the next road. This spell relies on the power of the four elements and the four directions, and it symbolises the crossing you are about to make. It will help to enhance all positivity for any kind of lifestyle change or new career direction.

What you will need:

white candle
turquoise (to represent air)

amber (to represent earth)
red jasper (to represent fire)
aquamarine (to represent water)

1. Place the white candle in the middle of a table. Place the turquoise to the east of it, the amber to the west of it, the jasper to the south of it and the aquamarine to the north of it.

2. Now light the candle and, with one finger, draw an imaginary circle around these compass points in a clockwise direction while you concentrate on your lifestyle change and what you want from it. Do this nine times (the number of empowerment).

3. Take a deep breath and blow out the candle. As you do so, all the goodness and positivity of the elements will radiate into the atmosphere, so put your hand out as if to welcome positive change.

4. Take up the crystals one by one. Hold them each for one minute and say: 'These crystals will empower me for positive change and the happiness I seek in my new direction.'

5. Place the crystals under your pillow or mattress and look forward to a fulfilling future.

Now that you know how to make magic work for you through spells and enchantments, let's take a visit into the world of psychic protection, power and dreams.

Chapter 4

Psychic Protection, Sixth Sense and Dream Interpretation

Your unconscious mind, which connects you to the universe, can help you discover more about the deeper aspects of your desires and goals, which often filter through into our sleeping world. Armed with a little psychic awareness, protection and the ability to understand the meaning of your dreams, you can combine these deeper insights with other practical work to make your life a magical one.

Psychic protection

Magic works best when we draw on the power of the universe to protect us from those things that we really don't want or need in our lives. These negative influences can be psychic or psychological invasion from others, external environmental influences or even nature itself. When we want to attract good things to us, we need to take care that we don't attract bad things to us too. The law of attraction works on the same magical principle that if you trust in the universe it will trust in you. But there is also negative energy out there, so before you can really begin to send out desires, wishes and wants, you also need some form of psychic protection.

Negative energy

There are many different types of negativity. It can come from other people: so-called friends, strangers, work colleagues, family or even your lover or partner, depending on their mood or psychological state. There is also external negative energy that is sometimes called 'geopathic stress'.

Geopathic stress is negative energy that derives from things like subterranean fault lines and water courses, overhead and underground electricity cables, pipelines, and even supernatural ley lines. The latter are straight paths or tracks which are believed to connect ancient sacred or pagan sites and have powerful electromagnetic energies that can disturb our own spiritual energy. Based on the laws of feng shui (the ancient Chinese art of harmony in the home and environment) there are also epicentres of difficult energy, such as static environments where the positive flow of energy is blocked; for example, you might live at the end of a cul-de-sac or on the middle floor of a tower block where energy becomes stagnant like a muddy pond.

How can you know what is bad energy in the environment? Here are some examples to give you an idea of what kind of stress, or not, you might be living with.

- Your home is surrounded by electrical overhead power lines (this energy is over-charged and there is too much power encroaching on you).
- You live next to a underground station or above it (this is rushing energy – highly stressful).
- You work or live in the middle floor of a tower block (energy is trapped and static – there's no flow).
- Home is at the end of a cul-de-sac or on a bend in a road where the destructive energy of traffic is constantly pointing straight towards your home as it passes by.
- High-rise obstacles, such as a line of tall poplar trees, are behind or in front of your home.
- There are tower blocks all around you.
- Radio beacons or strong street lighting are close to you, emitting electromagnetic waves.

Here are a few tips from feng shui on making your home a better place to live.

Outside

- A straight path from the road to the entrance to your home enables negative energy to flow easily towards your door. Try to break up the sharp energy of the straight line to your front door with potted plants, or get out your spade and give the path a few meanders.

- Satellite dishes on other people's homes, or bright lighting, generates highly charged energy. To counter this, place a mirror on the inside of your front door facing outwards to reflect and disperse negative energy.
- High-rise buildings deflect negative energy in your direction too. Use the same mirror trick as above.
- A small water feature near the front door is beneficial, as it calms all who enter.
- A low wall or hedge, or bushy plants near the front door, will all help to circulate positive energy.

Inside

- Avoid sleeping under heavy beams or facing an open door – both amplify negativity.
- In the office or at a desk, make sure you don't turn your back on the entrance. This will avoid direct negative energy stabbing you in the back.
- Always keep your loo seat down – to prevent money 'going down the drain' – unless you're literally sitting on it!
- Don't have your microwave facing you when you're sitting or eating, to avoid high-frequency energy, which can deplete your own.
- Hang or place a mirror on a wall opposite both back and front entrances to your home to deflect any negative energy when the doors are opened.

- Create a good balance of harmonious energy throughout the home using colour either in your decor or by including objects, plants or other forms of decoration that can represent similar qualities:

  Red for passion, love and enthusiasm
  Blue for spiritual calm, insight and contentment
  Yellow for good communication and family agreements
  Green for keeping you grounded, and for a sense of security and protection

- Include gold and silver for success, wealth and happiness in your home. You can use gold or silver objects as decoration – silver-framed mirrors, for example, or a gold-leaf or gold-coloured frame on a painting.

A protective magic space

To invite and enhance positive energy into your world, and for all those who enter your home, create a magic space in the entranceway. Although this space is invisible, you will know that each time you pass through, or anyone else for that matter, it will ground, calm, inspire, heal and attract happiness to you.

What you will need:

white quartz crystal

1. All you have to do is stand quietly for a few moments in your entrance hall or front door area. Then close your eyes, and, starting by facing the door, begin to draw a circle in the air with your finger as high and as wide as you can.

2. Now pivot slowly clockwise and draw seven more invisible circles in the air at each of the remaining seven main compass point directions, until you are facing back where you started. All these shapes are a sign that you have created this space specifically for the purpose of encouraging harmony in the home.

3. Once you have traced the outlines in the air, purify the space with a piece of white quartz crystal by leaving it in the entrance hall for a day and a night to amplify the atmosphere with beneficial energy.

4. Each time you pass through this space, remind yourself it's a welcoming shield for those who physically enter your home, and to attract good fortune and beneficial influences to you.

There are other ways to protect yourself and your home from difficult energy by the placement of crystals.

Crystals for home protection

According to feng shui practice, the eight compass directions, north, south, east, west, north-east, north-west, south-east and south-west, are all auspicious for various themes in your life. By placing a crystal associated with a specific theme, and in a specific area in the home, you will boost that area of your life and benefit from the crystal's harmonising and enhancing power; for example, a piece of malachite placed in the south-east corner of your home will improve your finances and help you to achieve prosperity. It will also protect you from anyone trying to undermine or stop you achieving what you want.

Added protection using crystals

You might feel that one area of your life is already under threat from negative energy; for example, you have a great job but are often laughed at by colleagues or you feel you'll never move on up the career ladder. In these instances, you would need to add a special 'stone protector' to the north area of your home too.

Below are the home areas, life themes and associated crystals. You can choose from several crystals to act as boosters and protectors as listed below, and if you feel already under threat, choose just one of the other listed stone protectors and place it in the part of the house where you need added protection.

The **south** is associated with success, fame, reputation and self-empowerment.

Crystals to boost and protect this area include: red carnelian, ruby and red tiger's eye.

The **south-west** is associated with marriage, romance and general happiness.

Crystals to boost and protect this area include: rose quartz, rhodochrosite and amethyst.

The **west** is associated with creativity, children, fertility and also the offspring of a fertile mind.

Crystals to boost and protect this area include: clear quartz, smoky quartz, opal and white topaz.

The **north-west** is to do with mentors, communication and new contacts.

Crystals to boost and protect this area include: calcite, yellow jasper, citrine and yellow fluorite.

The **north** is the epicentre of all career goals, achievement and professional interests.

Crystals to boost and protect this area include: green aventurine, emerald, peridot and jade.

The **north-east** is associated with wisdom, acceptance, education, learning and legal issues.

Crystals to boost and protect this area include: turquoise, blue lace agate, emerald and lapis lazuli.

The **east** is concerned with the family in general, the home and everyone's well-being.

Crystals to boost and protect this area include: onyx, jet, black tourmaline and smoky quartz.

The **south-east** is known as the 'wealth corner'. It is associated with prosperity, wealth and financial rewards.

Crystals to boost and protect this area include: malachite, jade and green tourmaline.

The protection stones

- **Amethyst** can be placed around the home as a general protection against electromagnetic fields and geopathic stress.
- **Black tourmaline** is the ultimate stone for all-round psychic protection. Place it in all the above areas to amplify and boost protective powers.
- **Onyx** protects and deflects negativity, and if worn, it maximises your own inner strength.
- **Shungite** and jet are both great protectors against other people's negative emotions.

Put any one of these stones in the area of your home where you feel most in need of a greater boost or extra support and protection.

Protect your secret desire and make it manifest

We all have secrets. Some of us aren't very good at keeping them, however, whereas others won't tell anyone anything (my lips are sealed!). Being so secretive can mean that we end up not having an easy life because our desire or secret longing hasn't been fulfilled, and so we become resentful of others. We create our own negative energy and sabotage our own secret desire in the process. How, then, can we protect and manifest our desires?

Here's how to protect yourself from negative influences while opening up your secret to the universe so that you can be rewarded with whatever it is you are truly seeking. Look through the list below, and if one of these desires speaks to you, obviously this deserves some magical attention.

1. A change of lifestyle
2. To have negotiating power
3. To enjoy a better sex life
4. For a successful business
5. To be beautiful
6. To be free
7. To be at one with the universe
8. To make a profit
9. To attract a new romance
10. For material achievement
11. For self-empowerment
12. To focus on a mission
13. To be centre stage

1. A change of lifestyle
Do you have a deep, hidden desire to revamp your lifestyle? To manifest your desire for change and to enable you to communicate or negotiate your plans, wear amber

during the day to protect yourself from other people's negativity and to improve your self-confidence. Place a piece of jasper in the north part of your home to activate your goals.

2. To have negotiating power

Do you want to improve you ability to make secret deals, effective negotiations or to resolve a problem? Place obsidian in the north-east corner of your living area to focus your thoughts. Wear or carry carnelian during the day to complete any deals or property negotiations. Place some small pieces of beryl in a terracotta bowl in your bathroom to promote the completion of a task.

3. To enjoy a better sex life

If you want a more dynamic sex life, wear or carry fire agate during the day to attract sexy interest and wear ruby when you go on dates. Place a piece of ruby in the south-west corner of the bedroom and also under your pillow to vitalise you and your partner's sexuality.

4. For a successful business

Do you secretly desire to make some new business contacts to get ahead? To align yourself with beneficial outside influences, and for successful communication, wear or carry a piece of lapis lazuli. To protect yourself from negative thoughts, place a piece of jade near to your front door. Every time you pass by, pick up the jade and hold it for a few seconds to imbue you with objectivity and discernment.

5. To be beautiful

Do you desire to be beautiful, more sensual and more attractive? Wear or carry moonstone and rose quartz during the day, and place both beneath your pillow at night. During the waxing moon, place both stones on a window ledge to align with fertile lunar energy, then remove and place under your pillow after the full moon to enhance your sensuality for the rest of the year.

6. To be free

Do you want to break free from someone or something that is stopping you from moving on? Carry or wear tiger's eye to balance your personal energy, and amber to dissociate yourself from negative people, bonds or situations. Place a piece of obsidian under your bed to strengthen your self-belief and your ability to move on.

7. To be at one with the universe

Do you have a secret desire to be simply joyful, happy or at one with the universe? Wear or carry a selection of turquoise, aquamarine and calcite. Turquoise opens you up to the endless possibilities of joy in the world, aquamarine gives you courage to find that joy, and calcite expands your awareness of joy and how it can operate in the simplest of ways in your life. You might soon discover that you find joy in simple things, such as seeing an old lady smile or hearing a bird singing.

8. To make a profit

Do you have a hidden desire to profit from business, take advantage of new opportunities, or climb the career or financial ladder? Place either a diamond (if you can afford a real one) or a piece of topaz in your work desk, drawer or in the area of your home where you do most of your work, to boost profitability. Carry or wear azurite on a daily basis to give you a clear head ready to seize any profitable opportunities.

9. To attract a new romance

Right now, is your deepest desire is to make a commitment, get married or find a new romance or soulmate? The three stones you need to wear or carry are garnet, sapphire and watermelon tourmaline. Garnets inspire romance, sapphires commitment and fidelity, and tourmaline, emotional and spiritual love. Place a garnet under your pillow to ignite intimacy, a sapphire in your living room to revitalise emotional warmth and compassion. To meet your soulmate, carry six garnets wrapped in a piece of paper for two full moons and your love will shortly appear after the second month.

10. For material achievement

Are you secretly driven to acquire success, wealth or anything associated with money and materialism? Luck will be even more on your side if you wear or carry citrine for abundance, sodalite to help you make intuitive decisions on financial opportunities and rhodochrosite to amplify self-confidence in your choices. To bring beneficial luck to your home, place six pieces of citrine in a small bowl and keep it by the front door. Each time you enter or leave, touch the stones and thank the universe for what is to come.

11. For self-empowerment
Do you secretly want to be less dependent on manipulative people, deceptions, negative emotions or abuse? Use these stones only for self-empowerment – not for power over others. To free yourself from the power others might have over you, wear or carry protective amethyst and shungite. To empower yourself, boost your confidence and free yourself from your vulnerability, also carry or wear bloodstone to give you courage and strength. Place three pieces of chalcedony in a box and put it under your bed to calm your emotions and help you to sleep better.

12. To focus on a mission
If you have a secret need to be more focused and objective, you can use onyx to enhance objectivity and reduce emotional investment in situations. Wear or carry onyx every day to help you concentrate and see the truth. Also, place carnelian on your desk or workplace to promote confidence and build a healthy sense of self-esteem.

13. To be centre stage
If you yearn to be centre stage, famous or adored by a large group of people, carry or wear a few pieces of rhodochrosite and fire agate to attract people towards you. Hematite will enable you to ground your plans, blue topaz

to manifest them, and blue lace agate to communicate them. Place two of each in a small pouch and put this in your desk or workplace to maximise your forthcoming success story and to protect you from envy and jealousy.

How to develop your psychic sense

Now that you know how to use crystals to help boost and protect your desires and home life, let's take a look at how you can develop your own sixth sense for healing and protection. Before doing any magic or spell work, we need some form of protection from external psychic energy and negative vibes that might be hanging around in the environment. To help us, we can utilise the invisible cloak of protection.

The following exercise is also useful if you need to go to an important meeting or interview – or even on a first date. You might need to protect yourself from other people's aggressive thinking, negative energy coming from colleagues, business contacts, the people on the bus, or when you enter a room full of unknown people, and so on. This wonderful protection technique can help you to feel positive and safe in any area of your daily or personal life.

Exercise: the magic cloak of protection

Here's how to cloak yourself with personal psychic power. When you first practise this technique, sit somewhere quiet, alone and where you won't be distracted by phones or people. Later, when you just need to throw on your cloak of protection as you go out of the house, or as you sit waiting for an important meeting, or go on a date, for example, you will just have to visualise wearing your cloak and – hey presto! – it will do its magic for you.

1. Sit somewhere quiet, rest your hands on your thighs and close your eyes.

2. Now, imagine a huge cloak billowing in the night sky against a backdrop of constellations and falling stars. Visualise this scene like a painting or a movie in your mind. Perhaps the cloak is even hanging from the edge of the crescent moon (yes, be imaginative; the more you dramatise and see every facet of this actual image, the better it will work for you). The cloak is probably enormous – as wide as a constellation and made of the most beautiful fabric, perhaps velvet, silk, taffeta, organza or a lush brocade. The cloak is covered in gold-spun threads and seems to be the most valuable, rich, beautiful and all-encompassing cloak you have ever seen.

3. Now decide what colour you want this cloak to be. Gold or silver perhaps? Or whatever colour you're currently passionate about: deep crimson, bright orange, or even black. It doesn't matter what colour you choose, it's your cloak, and because you are making it all your own, it is a very personal cloak of protection, and no one else can take it from you.

4. Next, visualise this cloak gradually falling down from the skies towards you. It billows and glides, soars and dives like a bird on the wing, and gradually, as it approaches earth, it begins to drop gold dust all around you. It falls

softly over your shoulders, around your body, your arms and legs, and it covers your head. The gold dust sprinkles over both you and the cloak, so you are a dazzling light in the sky just like the stars. But in fact, this cloak and its gold dust have made you invisible. Imagine as you stand up to look at yourself in a mirror you can neither see yourself nor the cloak. Now you are protected from all forms of negativity, even though no one can see you. You can walk out into the big wide world knowing that you are safe and protected by the cloak of the universe.

Put on this cloak whenever you feel you need protection.

Your psychic or sixth sense

According to the Greek philosopher Aristotle, we all have five known senses, and, of course, the equally known but usually misunderstood sixth sense, which is also known as intuition, ESP (extra-sensory perception), subtle perception ability, clairvoyance, and so on. This so-called sixth sense is actually made up of an array of different perceptive abilities. Therefore, we are just going to call it a 'psychic sense' – in other words, the ability to use your mind in a different way, one that opens the mind to the universe and allows us to reach the spiritual or soulful side of ourselves and that of others.

To develop this psychic sense, there are a few exercises below.

The first is to still the mind and to free yourself from the trappings of overthinking or incessant worrying, doubts and fears, and to connect to the spiritual realm, if you believe there is one.

The next two exercises are for developing your intuitive powers. These will enable you to be more aware of the areas of your mind that can intuit, or see, without having to use logic or to rationalise your actions. The right side of your brain is where imagination, intuition and enlightenment shine. (Logic, reason, and cause and effect are products of the left side of the brain.)

Whatever intuition is or isn't, there is a continuing open debate among scientists and occultists about what it might be. For the purposes of this book, we're going to side with the early 20th-century mystic Alice Bailey, who believed that it was the 'divine working though us' or, in other words, the universe itself making connections into which we suddenly log in. These are familiar to all of us, when we just know that something was meant to happen but don't know why. They were called moments of synchronicity by the great psychologist Carl G. Jung.

Before we can start to access this part of ourselves, we need to relax and still the mind.

Exercise: still your thoughts using mindfulness

To quieten the busy workings of the mind, most people resort to meditation – or what these days is often called mindfulness. Mindfulness is simply being aware of the present moment, in a way that calms the mind rather than allowing it to babble on incessantly.

Here's a simple step-by-step guide to an easy mindfulness technique. You don't have to do this every time you want to focus on using the tarot or other divination methods, but you will find it beneficial to use this method perhaps as part of a weekly ritual for relaxation and healing.

Stilling the mind can enrich you with a sense of being part of the universal magic itself, rather than splitting yourself off from it – in a way that I describe as: me-in-here-and-the-universe-out-there syndrome.

1. Sit somewhere quiet where you won't be interrupted. You can either sit cross-legged or on an upright chair with your hands resting on your thighs.

2. Close your eyes. Concentrate on your eyelids and how when they are closed they are filled with warmth and a dark glow of light. They are closed and soft, relaxed and unmoving. They are calm. They are not tightly closed, they are relaxed. They are already calming your mind.

3. Now turn your attention to the tips of your fingers of one hand as they rest on your thigh. Imagine your fingers are soft, warm, peaceful and totally relaxed. Feel the warmth in your fingers as an energy in itself.

4. Now this warm energy moves on up through your hand. Feel the muscles in your fingertips relax, and the warm, comforting feeling move slowly up into your other hand.

5. Gradually let the soft feeling move up through both your hands into your arms. It caresses your elbow joints, and then moves on up to your shoulders and neck. Now turn your attention to the warm energy as it moves into your feet and your toes. They too begin to rest and relax now. Feel the warmth of your toes and your feet in your mind.

6. As this warm energy moves on through your feet, your muscles relax. Your joints are softer, and this energy carries on moving up through your knees and up through your thighs, then it spreads across your lower body. You feel your body gradually relaxing, calm and peaceful. Lastly, let your chin drop a little towards your chest. Be aware of the relaxation, rather than allowing it to take over.

7. With your eyes still closed, start to concentrate on your breathing. Focus on your breath as you inhale through your nose and out, slowly through your mouth. Your in-breath will fill you with clear, purifying oxygen; your out-breath removes all tensions. Your breath is your life-force. It cleanses you, calms you and relaxes you. It fills you with healing power and allows you to arrive at the place of silence and stillness. Your in-breath is the door-way to positive well-being, good health and relaxation.

8. As you exhale through your mouth, you release all bodily tensions and all toxins. Feel the calmness of your breath as it gradually slows down, filling you with good-ness and releasing you from all stress.

9. If you find that you can't focus on your breathing for long, gently bring your attention back to it again. This may happen many times when you're starting mindfulness, but if you calmly tell your mind to focus again on your breath-ing, it will soon learn not to stray. As you develop more awareness of this power, you will find it easier to relax, your breathing will become deeper and you will soon arrive at the silent, still place. Be aware of your relaxed and calm state, and observe the tranquillity of your mind.

10. If you find that you're distracted by thoughts, let them pass by you. Let them pass through your mind; they are simply thoughts, nothing more. As you breathe softly and calmly, see these moments of thought as ripples on a still lake. They come and go; they are simply thoughts that enter your mind and leave again.

11. Now gently focus your attention on an image of a tree. Concentrate on the tree. Notice the colour of the tree trunk, the texture of the bark. Is it rough or smooth? Is the trunk old and wrinkled, or smooth and shiny? Be aware of the leaves, their size, colour and their shape. See the veins of each leaf; focus on the tree, both its details and then as a whole tree. Does it spread out its branches like a great oak or rise up like a straight poplar? This focus will help you to stay in the moment. Keep focusing, keep thinking of the tree in your mind.

12. As you concentrate your mind on the tree, you will discover another part of your mind that becomes aware of that very concentration. You may also become aware of distractions. You might hear sounds outside, birds singing, traffic passing. You may feel uncomfortable in your chair, or feel an itch that you want to scratch. Be aware of these things, but don't be put off concentrating on the tree. Keep turning your attention gently back to the image of the tree as you drift into the meditative state.

13. Keep concentrating on the tree in your mind. You are now gradually arriving at a mindful, meditative state. Gently allow the image of the tree to fade away now. It is as if the tree is getting smaller and smaller. It is as if the colours are fading into nothing and you see only a

vague, misty ghost of a tree, and then it's gone from view and there is nothing in your mind. There is no image, no sound, no thought, there is nothing. Now you will find yourself in the silent place even if only for a few seconds, or minutes.

14. Gently come back to normality by opening your eyes.

You are now ready to do any kind of magical or healing work, armed with your invisible cloak of protection.

Next, to develop your intuitive powers try out these two fun-and-easy exercises.

Exercise: develop your intuition

We all have hunches. We might think, perhaps, *if I go via that route there will be less traffic*, and so we do. And, lo and behold, no traffic – yes! I was right! Or, *I know I'm going to bump into my ex today – I just feel it*. Then you do. Give these hunches and feelings a chance: make a plan to follow up on your hunches on one specific day, all day.

1. One simple way to develop this is to imagine the exact parking place before you get to where you are going to go and park. As you are driving along, see the empty space in your mind. You can see the road, the space, a car just leaving and a gap that opens up.

2. As you get nearer, keep seeing this empty space and really believe in what your mind is seeing. This is the intuitive part of your brain at work. If you do find the space when you get there, you'll know that your intuition is beginning to work its own magic for you.

Exercise: improve your intuition – the oracle

This is a simple exercise that gives you a choice – whether you believe it's entirely random or not is another matter. But what matters is that at the moment you choose the oracle (in other words, an ambiguous message you later find has significance) it will have meaning in your life for the rest of the day. Here, your intuitive powers will come into force as you make connections all day long. Here's how to do it:

1. First thing in the morning, take a book, randomly, from your bookshelves – perhaps close your eyes or just run your finger along a line of books, then choose one. Or choose a magazine or newspaper, or just look on the internet at a series of random images – close your eyes and point somewhere on the screen.

2. If you chose the book method, turn the book pages idly until you stop at one page, and then without looking, idly move your finger over the page until you point your finger to one place. Whatever the sentence reads, this is going to be crucial to your intuitive day; for example, your random line might say something apparently meaningless such as, 'he was the chairman of the board.' Or something more fascinating like, 'the wind began to whistle through the trees.' Get the picture?

3. However you happen upon this random choice of words or image (although in the world of magic nothing is random as such – we call it synchronicity), keep the image in your mind for the rest of the day, and see how many times something unexpected actually is strangely coincidental with this special sentence. Write it down so that

you don't forget it, and you will start to let your intuition bridge the gap between thought and action.

Now let's move on to another facet of the mind: our dream world.

Dreams and their meanings

It's quite a mental battle to sort out our intuition from the workings of our imagination sometimes, isn't it? Did we imagine the lottery ticket numbers we wanted to win, or did we use our intuition to choose them? If you read the section on developing your intuition, you'll know there's a fine line between intuition and imagination, and both are often dependent on one another. Our dream world is another area that holds a mysterious fascination over us, especially as it seems we have very little control over it.

The brain, according to one school of thought, processes a load of unimportant or useless mental material that gets dumped at the end of the day into the recesses of our mind, some of which gets filtered into bizarre or theatrical random connections. It's these mind games that we call our dreams.

Another school of thought believes that however dreams are processed, they are insights into our unconscious, or even our universal, mind. Correctly interpreted they can tell us an awful lot about ourselves. This sort of psychological approach is the one that we're going to follow, but with a little touch of magic thrown in.

The magic of dreams

What is magical about dream work? Dreams can help us to understand our true desires, our true needs, our fears or woes, our regrets, and so on. If magic is a way of making things happen, we can do this by listening to and interpreting our dreams. We can then manifest our unconscious desires or live out the true potential of our character in the big wide world. We can also accept and then heal the inner workings of ourselves.

Dreams reveal amazing secrets about particular aspects of our personal psychology, but they are also linked to our imagination – our fantasy world. Sometimes things that are imagined, added to random threads of our daily life, are shaped into the dream picture and then become mixed up with the other information hidden in our unconscious that perhaps we need to know about.

Therefore, we have to break through the confused imagery of the dream to get to the heart of the ancient symbols that are carried in what Jung called 'the collective unconscious'. These are motifs and symbols he called 'archetypes', which are common to everyone throughout every culture and civilisation around the world. We'll be looking at these symbols in the tarot section, but they also tell us the basic truths about our jumbled dreams.

Dream meanings

For our dream meanings we are going to stick mostly to a mixture of interpretations derived from both a psychological approach and a magical one. After all, if the unconscious is sending us messages through our dreams, like any oracle we need to try to understand it; however, we can't all traipse off to the psychoanalyst to get our lives sorted, can we? With a little help, however, we can at least try to shape our deepest desires and needs around the here and now of life.

The magic of dreams will help you to understand yourself, and heal or bring to life those dormant longings or desires. Depending on your viewpoint, it may or may not help you to predict the future, but it will enhance your self-awareness for that future.

A brief introduction to dream interpretations

The following interpretations are based on psychological motifs, ancient symbolic archetypes and magical associations. Adapt them according to your own lifestyle.

ENVIRONMENT

Buildings/houses Dreaming of a house or home is meant to represent the different aspects of yourself. Depending on the state of the house – its size, layout and what levels it includes – the dream symbolises various states of mind or current physical needs:

- The **loft** suggests that perhaps you have too many ideals or lofty thoughts.
- The **bedroom:** is it cosy, or cold and unwelcoming? The sensation you feel reveals how you feel about yourself.
- The **roof** represents high aspirations, or ideas that need to be grounded.

- The **basement** represents the unconscious and how you may need to explore your feelings, emotions and needs.
- A **ruined house** suggests that you are coming to the end of one cycle of your life, and it's time to let go and move on to somewhere new, either in a relationship or literally out there in the big wide world. Let go.
- An **unfinished or new house** is a symbol of being motivated to get cracking with your goals.
- A **windowless house** means that you need to put in windows to open you up to a new perspective. Alternatively, you may now be ready to build a new life and explore opportunities.
- A **strange, rambling, or eerie house** symbolises an unconscious need to reveal unknown facts about yourself, even if they are scary. It also symbolises hidden truths about the past, which if brought to light, can bring positive results.
- The **garage** is a modern-day interpretation of delving into what your sexual needs are really all about.
- A **palace or castle** symbolises that you have great aspirations to achieve something or to change your lifestyle.
- A **stable** symbolises security and control. This is a time when you can confidently harness your strengths and use them to your advantage.
- A **tower** is, according to Sigmund Freud (the founder of psychoanalysis), a male phallic symbol.

Enjoy! More recent interpretations include a feeling of isolation, trapped by one's fears, or a desire for retreat from the world.

- A **farm** symbolises that you might be hoping for a simpler, rustic lifestyle, or a secret desire to move to the country.

LANDSCAPES

- A **mountain** can represent an enormous challenge ahead of you and, depending on how you view the mountain, whether you are ready to conquer it or not. If viewed from a valley, it might include a fear of the impossibility of the task ahead. If you're standing on top of a mountain, however, you've reached the peak and feel satisfied with all that you've achieved.
- A **meandering river** usually represents the ability to adapt and go with the flow or a willingness to make some important changes. A **fast-flowing rushing torrent** symbolises that there are many obstacles ahead, but that you're ready to accept the changes and test the waters.
- A **valley** is a symbol of abundance; wide lush valleys reveal you have creative or fertile thoughts that need expression or that your feelings are going to be rewarded.
- A steep-sided **gorge** leading down to a crevice-like valley is said to represent a sexual adventure ahead, but one where you will discover more about your sexual needs too.

- The vastness of a **desert** indicates a need to see the bigger picture and that there is more to be seen than meets the eye, or it is time to take a new perspective on an old problem.

- The **sea** is the archetypal symbol of the Great Mother and female sexuality. Depending on what is happening to you in the dream, here are some examples: nearly drowning or being underwater denotes that you have deep-seated fears about how to deal with reality; floating or swimming happily points to enjoying your sex life and being able to accept the ebb and flow of events.

- Traditionally, like the sea, a **lake** is a symbol of female sexuality. Floundering in a lake means that you are confused about life and love; floating serenely on a lake means that you are happy with your sex life.

- Like the sea, a **flood or tsunami** symbolises the archetypal Great Mother. This can mean that you are overwhelmed by feelings of responsibility either to family, partner or work, or simply that you feel submerged in the pressures of life.

- An **island** represents a safe place. Dreaming you are on an island suggests that you are content with your life, or if you feel a sense of unease at being there, that you fear moving on. On the other hand, if you are seeking an island, or you come across one in your dream travels, your search for peace and security is of importance right now.

ELEMENTS

- **Heavy rain** is often interpreted as a sign that you feel you can't complete a project or you're inundated with duty or choices. If you dream of **light rain**, you are gradually making progress with your goals.

- A blanket of **snow** across a landscape symbolises pure thinking and perfect thoughts, and can lead to good results. A bleak snowstorm symbolises that you are covering up your warm feelings with cold words or actions.

- Large cumulus-type **clouds** indicate a worry or anticipation of things to come, whereas a totally white cloud-covered sky symbolises that being stubborn is preventing you from experiencing fresh insight.

- **Storms** symbolise your own moods, including anger and frustration. You may feel tossed between a whirlwind of changing feelings, caught in a tornado of passion, whether love or hate, and torn by the disparity of needs and desires.

- **Thunder** represents that you might be in fear of an authority figure or anxiously awaiting a challenge, a test or a difficult task.

- Fork **lightning** represents a sudden flash of insight or brilliant thinking. It can also symbolise that right now inspiration is needed to resolve a creative issue.

- An **earthquake** symbolises that sexual passions are awakened or that repressed feelings are engulfing you with worry; however, the earth-quake also indicate that this is a time to let powerful creative energy come through to your conscious world. (See also **flood or tsunami** in the list under Landscapes above.)

- As a symbol of redemption and spiritual promise, the **rainbow** is also a sign of imminent achievement, optimism and enlightenment.

- **Sunshine** – dreams of bright sunlight can represent your growing self-awareness, an ability to know what life-direction or what vocation is right for you, or a sunny day can simply signify happy times ahead.

- A **full moon** symbolises the realisation of how to utilise your own personal magic to complete a quest, goal or project. A **crescent moon** points to a fresh start or beginning that will set you on the road to happiness.

ANIMAL LIFE

- Insects with wings, such as **butterflies**, tend to reveal a need to go away and rethink your priorities and then to come back to the reality of a situation; the **moth** shows that, like the burning flame it's attracted to, careful thought is needed before rushing into a hot situation.

- On one level the **spider** signifies a powerful mother or feminine influence in your life, who might be controlling you. If in the dream you fear the spider, this indicates a fear of being trapped, a fear of taking responsibility, or that you are stuck in a difficult situation.

- A **deer** represents a desire to return to innocence or to stay beyond reproach; a herd of deer suggests a feeling that it's time to remain peaceful in moments of stress.

- A solitary **wolf** indicates that you are currently alone or need to be alone to fulfil a mission or goal. If you are fearful of wolves, your own desires are not compatible with your needs. Being chased by a wolf symbolises that you are not ready to take on responsibility for your actions.

- All predators are scary in dreams and suggest a time to face our fears. Being chased by a **tiger** is about being scared of your long-term goals or grand schemes. Will they ever manifest? But if you meet and converse with a noble or calm tiger, this indicates that you are about to make a stand for what you believe in.

- The **snake** in most civilisations has been identified as a symbol of either evil or sexuality. For the purposes of modern-day dreams, let's equate it with sexual power. When you dream of a snake or a serpent, it's timely to affirm your sexual needs, or you're in need of a sexual partner. Evil? Well, I guess the idea of some form of guilt raises its head if you dream of a cobra!

- In Chinese astrology, the **rat** is considered a noble animal that gets ahead, does things, and is strategic and highly intelligent. In dreams it represents your ability to sort out your life and be one step ahead of the rest. Popping up from the dark drains and watery underworld he inhabits, the rat can also symbolise that you are ready to reveal a secret to someone.

- Like the tiger, all **cats** are notorious for being independent, self-assured and the power behind every throne. Cat dreams are associated with self-improvement, authority and progress.

- The **dog** is a pack animal like the wolf. But dreaming of gentle, docile or obedient dogs is associated with your need to be more laid-back about life. Dreams involving aggressive dogs prompt you to realise how difficult you can be sometimes or that someone in your life is angry and needs to communicate their feelings honestly.

- Reining in a **wild horse** is not for the faint hearted, only for the intuitive or well-schooled trainer. This is a wild animal that flies in the face of danger. You too either want to gallop away from a difficult situation if you have wild-stallion-type dreams, whereas a grazing horse, a training one, or an easy ride, points to your readiness to learn self-control and to manifest your ideas.

- **Birds** are a sign of our unconscious desire to be liberated from the earthbound form we inhabit. On a more daily level, you might feel trapped by your lifestyle and want to change it; you may worry that you don't have enough space in a relationship, or you may need to spread your wings and fly.

- Slippery as they may be, most psychologists believe that **fish** are symbols of sexuality. Dreaming of a shoal of fish can denote that you are overwhelmed by possible lovers – how nice! Being a fish symbolises a need to understand your sexual needs; to see a fish floundering in water or being caught might suggest that you may be confusing idealistic romantic love with pure physical lust.

PEOPLE

We all dream of friends, both past and present, as well as lovers, and even strangers we've never met. Sometimes we dream of them because we've just met up with them, or wish we could meet them; sometimes we even dream of them and then randomly bump into them the next day. That is one of the magical elements of dreams, where whether you believe in dream prediction or just synchronicity, dreams enable us to reach down into our unconscious world and traverse the bridge to universal knowledge.

In most psychological circles all these people are considered to be aspects of ourselves, or are symbolic of something about our relationships with these people.

- Dreaming of **friends**, or that you are enjoying good company, suggests that you are ready to chill out and take a break from hard work. A friendly soirée or party indicates that you're feeling good about yourself and confident enough to make the right contacts to improve your lifestyle. Dreaming that friends are strangers or are blanking us suggests a lack of self-confidence, or that specific people are actually of little value in our lives.

- How often do you dream of a **stranger** – a dark horse, a mysterious, unknown lover? The one who you've always fantasised about, but never really met in real life? Perhaps this person is a heroic or dramatic character who sweeps you off your feet? You can't quite see their face, but you respond to their touch, voice or just the fact that they are a stranger to you. Dreaming of a passing stranger, say on a train for example, can indicate that you need to venture forth or get out of a rut; the lover–stranger dream reveals that you may be searching for an ideal that doesn't exist, or if you prefer a more spiritual interpretation, that somewhere out there in the universal web, you have a soulmate.

- There are two ways of looking at **mother** dreams. One is from the psychological viewpoint where any dreams of mother (whether your own, the archetypal Mother Earth, or being a mother yourself) indicate sexual completion, life-giving energy and containment. But just dreaming about one's own physical mother often reveals issues we have had in the past with her, or which still need clarification depending on how you react or feel in the dream towards her and how she appears to react to you.

- Similarly, dreams of your **father** can be interpreted in several ways. From a Jungian perspective, the father is a symbol of authority, power and male sexuality. Like the Emperor in the tarot, dreams of your father might be associated with a need to find one's own inner authority or to rely more on masculine energy or power to get results. Alternatively, dreaming of one's own father simply brings to light your current feelings towards him and any issues that have yet to be resolved. How do you feel when you meet him in your dreams? How does he talk to you?

- The archetypal **wise old man or guru** appears in dreams when you may need guidance or good advice. This is a time for personal development and becoming more mature about yourself or your work

- If you accept and identify with the **naked people** around you in your dream, this can signify that you are happy with the way others act or behave and feel that they are open and honest enough to be trusted. If you are naked, too, then this confirms your ability to not fear what others think about you. If however, you don't accept other people's nudity or you find it offensive, you probably resent someone's openness. If you're naked and feel guilty or exposed – you're still dominated by your own psychological inhibitions, you have not found it in you to be completely confident in revealing your own character. This dream suggests that it's timely to come clean or to bare your thoughts.

In magic, dreaming of **mythical or historical characters**, as wide-ranging as Cleopatra, William the Conqueror, Aphrodite or Picasso, not only informs us of our own specific issues, but it can also be a sign that we can now express inspirational or creative ideas reaped from the universe itself. Obviously there are thousands of mythical people, archetypal characters and real-life historical ones. Two types are listed below.

- **Hero/heroine types** – Odysseus, Lancelot, Achilles, Hercules, Einstein, Mother Teresa, Psyche, Joan of Arc, Artemis, Freya – whether in myths, fiction, or those who have lived, are usually people who are trying to redeem themselves from some real or perceived failing, either in their character or from previous deeds. They are on a quest, and at the end of the quest they acquire profound wisdom, not only about themselves but also about life itself.

  When we dream of these kinds of heroes we are being reminded that if we want to become heroic in some way (to save others, fight for a belief, rise above all challenges, and so on) there is a price to pay, and that is that we must come down from

our ivory tower and see our own truth; we have
to accept our own flaws before we can realistically
hope to be the hero of our dreams.

- **Villain types** in a dream — Medusa, Medea,
Circe, Hecate, Hades, Hitler, Stalin, Macbeth,
Genghis Khan — represent our own dark urges.
We all have what Jung called a 'shadow side' and
this latent part of ourselves usually only dares to
set foot in our apparent real world through our
dreams, reminding us that all human beings are
capable of evil intentions, and some live them out
in the most horrifying way. These villainous characters appear in our dreams when we need to look
carefully at our true motives for doing what we do.

Doing things

- One of the most liberating and seemingly out-of-
this-world type of dream, **flying** through the air
unaided by wings, planes or any kind of carrier is
an experience of pure elation and is never forgot-
ten. Interpreting this dream has many variations.
Psychologically it indicates you are at one with
the universe or have experienced the immortal
or divine soul of yourself. On other levels it suggests the following: you are beginning to find the
freedom of self or creativity you seek; you need
to take a larger perspective on life; you want to
liberate yourself from material bonds; or that life
isn't so bad now that you know you can rise above
it and beyond the physical body.

- Most dreams of **journeys** indicate a need to move on, to change, to progress and to motivate yourself towards a new beginning or direction. After all, if life is a journey and not a destination, we are always moving along one road or another. Dreams of journeys are simply reminders of that life pathway, and that you need to map it out, check out the signposts and follow the path that has meaning for you. When I say meaning, I am referring to a sense of adventure, vocation or a calling, in whatever direction that will take you.

- If you are **driving a car** and have no care in the world, this dream suggests you're ready for a new departure as long as you are in the driving seat. If you are a back-seat driver, you need to make it clear to others that you either have to put your trust in them or you won't go for the ride.

- Are you dreaming of **journeys by foot** – solitary hiking, or wandering lonely as a cloud? How you are walking is irrelevant, but the surrounding landscape or the destination in sight might give you clues to the issues involved in the dream. This is obviously a time for introspection and reflection on your life journey. Open roads are symbols of freedom; meandering paths or obstacles along the way represent the need to move on but with the realisation that it won't be easy.

- Arriving at **crossroads** in any journey dream indicates a need to make an important life-changing decision or choice. You may have to leave behind something or someone you love because this part of your life will mean letting go of the past. This can be a relationship change, a career move or a desire to live a long way from home.

- **Falling** dreams are very common, in that they suggest you may feel insecure about the direction you're going in or the responsibility you're about to undertake. You may be unsure of yourself and the claims you have made, or you might need to be more realistic about your goals and expectations.

- Sometimes our dreams involve that horrid feeling that, as much as we try to climb up a slippery slope or drive up a steep road, we keep **slipping or sliding backwards**. This is an alert, telling us to not turn into a control freak and that sometimes we have to let go and listen to other people or let them take the helm. Alternatively, it might symbolise that you have taken on more than you are capable of and you need to just take a back seat for a while.

- Whether **climbing** a mountain, a hill, cliff-face or molehill, if the end in sight seems a long way off, or the climb strenuous and hard, reaching your goal is not an easy one to obtain. We may be expecting too much of ourselves, or that others have higher expectations of us than we are capable of achieving.

- Unpleasant dreams of **drowning** in the sea, or

being overcome by tsunami-like waves, reveal we may need to come to terms with our greatest fears, or at least let them see the light of day. Being conscious of what you fear helps you to face it, and drowning suggests you are floundering in emotional waters, rather than rising above the waves or surfing to the shore.

- If you are **running away** from someone or something unpleasant, you aren't ready to face up to your responsibilities. If you are eagerly **running towards** something or someone, this dream indicates your impatience to get your priorities sorted out, and no one is going to stop you.

- Dreaming of **restraint**, as in any kind of chained experience, such as being bound, held captive, kidnapped, bound and gagged, and so on, suggests that you are blind to your own desires or needs, or are fearful of failure. Perhaps you are holding back from an important move forward. Alternatively, other people might be holding you responsible for their unhappiness, making you feel guilty by projecting their plight on to you.

- Once thought to be a symbol of a huge sexual appetite, **eating your favourite food** in a dream indicates your desire for a more erotic sex life. **Eating something distasteful**, however, symbolises that you haven't yet made your sexual needs clear to someone, or you just don't really fancy the physical aspects of a relationship.

- **Losing teeth** is a well-known and often recurring dream in many people's lives, suggesting a fear of losing one's vitality or sexual prowess. But perhaps it more commonly reflects a deep-seated fear of growing old and leaving behind one's childlike exuberance.

- **Sex** – erotic dreams are simply that: erotic. And they can disturb or delight us physically when graphic sexual imagery or a complete sensual experience wakes us up in a state of orgasmic lust. Dreaming of passionate lovemaking, erotic turn-ons, sexual fantasies, and even red roses, can also be associated with an intense need for creative or artistic expression. In fact, sexuality and creativity are bound inextricably together. Sexual activity may need to be replaced with creative expression, or vice versa.

- Going on a **shopping** trip can be the ultimate retail-therapy dream! We know it works in practice, so why not in the imaginary world of the mind? We can see all the possibilities and opportunities before our eyes. What a joy to be able to have everything that we want! However, getting frustrated while shopping, or being bustled by annoying crowds or not finding what you are looking for (even if you don't know what that is but are just looking anyway), all indicate that we may be unable to fulfil all our goals or that we can't get what we truly want out of life. With all shopping dreams, perhaps it's time to prioritise the actual shopping list – so, if you haven't made one, make it now.

- Most dreams that include **violent acts** in one form or another, whether to oneself or towards another, indicate that it's time to deal with one's own pent-up anger or frustration. There are often deeper unconscious drives and issues that need resolving, too, so treat these dreams with respect but don't fear them – they are just trying to tell you to accept and work with your dark or shadow side (we can't always live in the light).

ASPECTS OF OURSELVES

- Dreams of **fame**, seeing your name in lights, or of being centre stage or having celebrity status, indicate that you are in need of more self-esteem so that you can be ready to go out there and shine. This kind of dream often occurs when you are feeling particularly ambitious for new challenges and are ready to make a name for yourself in some way unique to you.

- Although fame is **success**, success isn't always fame, so if you dream of being successful in any enterprise, project or goal, the likelihood is that you very soon will be. But it takes self-belief and an understanding that you have to make success happen; like magic, it doesn't just fall into your lap because you dreamt it.

- When we dream of **failure**, we feel weak and vulnerable. We feel like we've lost the race or are lacking in potential and are inadequate in some way. Dreaming of failing an exam, losing a game, having a communication breakdown or simply not being able to live up to our own expectations suggests we need to understand our own limitations, and not reach for the stars when we can't even touch the moon.

- **Feeling frustrated** by events, people, or even our own clumsiness, is a sign in dreams that we need to pay more attention to our true potential rather than trying to prove something to others. Dreams that have a constant theme of frustrated events — not getting somewhere on time, being rejected by others, not finishing a project, running out of time, getting stuck in a traffic jam, computer not working, people not phoning when you thought they would — are signs that you are always being thwarted in your desires and that it's time to understand if those desires are actually in tandem with your true potential.

- Like dreaming of beautiful strangers, heroes or heroines, knights in shining armour or damsels in distress, dreams that involve a **romantic relationship** are powerful signs that either it's missing in your life right now or that you are about to embark on a new affair. If partnered, and you dream of having an intense love affair with someone else, this can indicate a secret betrayal of your partner. It could be that either you can't help yourself from being attracted to another person or the dreams are just cheeky fantasies of the mind, the well-known 'what if?' illusion. Dreams of losing or being left by your partner, lover or new admirer are usually based on insecurity and a lack of self-confidence. The dream suggests you might need to develop your self-esteem and independent spirit so that your relationship is on an equal basis.

- There are so many **fear** dreams that just the theme of fear itself should be enough to work with. In fact, strange beasts, dark shadows of the night, looming evil, being followed, disaster-movie-type dreams, and so on, all have one thing in common, and that's the fear of 'being' – living in fear of the inevitable death of one's physical body. These kinds of dreams are often frequent if you have no spiritual or soulful connection to the universe. Living without fear is almost impossible, but accepting that life is for living every day to the best of your ability, is one step towards slaying these mares of the night so that you can dream instead of the elation of living. Perhaps fear dreams are a sign that it's time to dream of flying and the liberation from fear itself?

- Dreaming of **loss** can be anything from a favourite book to the loss of a loved one, either through death, betrayal or just bad luck. But the loss is felt acutely in the dream, as if you have been left with nothing or lost a part of yourself. You may literally have lost something or someone, but often this sense of loss indicates that you might have lost your sense of direction in life: feeling abandoned by the one you've lost – having to accept that what is lost has gone, and that it's time to move on.

- There are many dreams that revolve around **seeking or looking for something or someone** – a deep desire to find or discover, or to go on some kind of quest. When in the dream you know what it is you are seeking, this is a sign that you're on the right pathway for your life journey right now. If you are aimlessly wandering around not knowing what you are looking for, but know there is something or someone out there, this represents your urge to find a new direction.

There are many other dream themes, but unfortunately we don't have room in this little book to look at them all. Remember, what you dream is who you are, and who you are is part of the magic of the universe.

From learning about the world of psychic protection, imagination and dreams, you can also learn to practise the art of divination, the subject of the next chapter.

Chapter 5

The Magic of Divination

Ever wondered how to truly plot or plan your future? Do you often struggle to make decisions, or are you happy to embrace change or adapt to what seems like fate – in other words, external events or influences that come into your life? Perhaps you are one of those people who secretly reads your daily horoscope, has an occasional visit to a fortune teller or reads your tarot cards online? If so, this chapter is for you. It dips into practical divination – or how to take control of your destiny and the magic of manifesting your desires.

Before you make your magic happen, you need to know what those desires are and whether they are truly yours, and not those plonked in your head by your family, our culture, your generation, or your lovers or pals. We often think we want more than anything in the world to be free and independent, or we think we really want to parent five beautiful kids and cook amazing meals for an adoring partner. This might be what we *think*, but it isn't always in tandem with our deepest *desires* or *true potential*. Learning about yourself through astrology or the other forms of divination covered in the next chapter – numerology, reading the tarot or interpreting palms – are key ways towards discovering more about your personal pathway and true desires. Working with the tools of the divination trade will also help you to make the right decisions to make your future how you truly want it to be.

The magic and art of divination

There are two keys to divination: your own intuitive or psychic powers, and the tools you use to help you access universal magic. Before you throw yourself into tarot reading or discover your vocational pathway with the help of astrology, let's look more closely at what the magic of divination actually is.

What does divination mean?

The word 'divination' comes from the word 'divine', which is rooted in an ancient word meaning 'to be inspired by the gods'. In other words, frankly, whether you believe in them or not, when you are divining the future, you're getting in touch with the gods, or the guardians of the storehouse of universal knowledge.

A storehouse of knowledge is a bit far-fetched isn't it? No. Let's use an analogy. It's a bit like an infinite library of every book ever written or that will be written. These books reveal past, present and future. In fact, it was thought by some ancients, such as the Egyptians and Mesopotamians, that this storehouse of knowledge was the secret language of the gods. Today, we could rephrase this and say that these gods and their books are simply symbolic of the archetypes carried in the collective human psyche. Each of us carries and can access this secret store-house of information locked away in our unconscious.

When we read the future, we are digging deep within ourselves via our unconscious universal self, aided by a few key elements 'out there'. These can be the patterns of planets in the sky (astrology), symbolic images and mir-rors (tarot) and other key imagery such as palm lines, and powerful numbers, to name but a few.

This is the art (using techniques and tools) and magic (using the universal energy within ourselves) of discovering how to manifest our desires and live the future we want.

The rule of engagement

Like everything in the world of magic, when engaging in the art of divination, it's important to be very aware of projecting facets of your character, either on the interpret-ation or the outcome of a situation.

'Know thyself' is a line from the Greek god Apollo's sacred temple. Before you read anyone else's chart, palm, tarot, numbers, runes or whatever, remember that you will undoubtedly project your own agenda (whether con-scious or unconscious) on to that other person. Be aware of how you judge the tarot card's qualities, and try to keep an open mind, a non-judgemental attitude and a clear vision undistorted by your perception; for example, to you, the card Death might make you uncomfortable because you hate change (this is its major meaning), so you're likely to project that feeling of fear on to that card without seeing it with an open mind. Yet for someone else, change might be very welcome.

Let's start with astrology. It's a big subject, but with a few simple basics you can learn to understand what your life journey is all about and aim to seal your goals and expectations in accordance with that pathway.

A sense of calling

Have you ever felt the sense of vocation that some people talk about? A feeling so strong within that you just have to follow that pathway? Most of us don't, because we've had it washed out of us, repressed, denied or suppressed by our interaction with the environment and life itself. If you don't know what your calling or vocation is, astrology can put you right back on that pathway.

The magic of astrology and the horoscope

A mix of art and science, astrology has been around for thousands of years and is the precursor of modern-day astronomy. Eons ago, the magi of ancient civilisations looked up to the stars and planets and saw interesting patterns in the sky. These patterns, when repeated over and over again seemed to reflect similar events on earth; for example, when the moon was full, the tides were high, hares ran wild across the hillsides and lovers got emotional. When the 'morning star' (Venus) was at its brightest, women were more seductive; when Mars, the 'red planet', was very close and it looked even redder, war was in the air; and solar eclipses seemed to resonate with doom for some kings, or winning, to the loser's rival!

It was by watching the planets and the sun and moon as they moved through the sky, apparently orbiting the earth (the fact that the sun was the centre of the solar system came a lot later), led to a belief that what happened up there reflected or mirrored what happened down here on earth. Why or how was not that relevant, but it seemed to be that the planets were direct mouthpieces of the gods themselves and so were identified directly with specific qualities of that god.

The earliest celestial observations were linked with the art of interpreting and divining the future from the stars. In pre-Christian times, this was more to do with predicting future events, politics, wars, famine, weather, and so on. It wasn't until the classical period (in Europe at least) that individual horoscopes began to be cast, and it was seen that the individual had his or her own physical behaviour, and even future, written in the stars, too.

This is the time when other correspondences were recognised, like the ones we saw in the first chapter. Red equated to Mars, to a ruby, to blood, to the state of one's blood, to war, to courage, to valour, and so on. Individual birth charts, therefore, were not like our modern-day interpretations where we might say, 'Oh, he's a Gemini so he's a bit of a kid at heart.' More that this man with a powerful Mercury in his chart is fleet-footed and as tricky as Mercury/Hermes (the sign ruler). Both the god and the planet were interchangeable.

The horoscope

The horoscope comes from ancient Greek words meaning 'observing the moment'. It is made up of the ecliptic (the 360-degree apparent path of the sun as it moves around the earth) divided into 12 imaginary slices (each slice is 30 degrees). These slices are known as the 12 signs of the zodiac. The signs are grouped into four elements, the three quadruplicities, also known as qualities, and the 12 houses.

The signs of the zodiac

The word 'zodiac' means 'animal figures', and the zodiac signs get their names from the constellations that were first perceived by the magicians of ancient Mesopotamia. As the sun apparently moved around the earth, it appeared to travel across a background of 12 constellations. These became associated with the sun's pathway throughout the year, divided into twelve 30-degree segments of a 360-degree circle, as mentioned above. Each segment was named after the relevant constellation. In modern astrology, when the sun 'moves through' one of these twelve zodiac signs, the sign is known as a sun sign.

In ancient Greek and Roman times, each sign of the zodiac was assigned a ruling planet or god; however, the planets Uranus, Neptune and Pluto were only discovered in the last few centuries, so prior to this there were only seven known planets (in Western astrology) ruling twelve signs. In those days, Jupiter ruled Sagittarius and Pisces, Saturn ruled Capricorn and Aquarius, and Mars ruled Aries and Scorpio.

Nowadays the following planets are the rulers in Western astrology.

The zodiac signs and their rulers

Aries – Mars

Taurus – Venus

Gemini – Mercury

Cancer – the moon

Leo – the sun

Virgo – Mercury

Libra – Venus

Scorpio – Pluto

Sagittarius – Jupiter

Capricorn – Saturn

Aquarius – Uranus

Pisces – Neptune

Astrological correspondences

If you look back to the 12 Magic Crystals section starting on page 21 of Chapter 1, you will see some of the correspondences that tie in with astrological qualities for these signs, as well as those for the crystals; for example, if you think about the sun sign Leo, then you're also associating (deep down inside if not consciously) the sun, light, gold, sunstone, tiger's eye, bold, ego-centred, creative, glowing, centre of attention, showy, pushy, stubborn, proud, lions.

Using this Leo sign example, all Leo traits and characteristics have a certain flavour about them, and, similarly, other signs have their own unique associations, too. Try this exercise to stretch your mind to zodiac heights.

Exercise: working with the zodiac
What you will need:

    pen
    paper

1. Write down each sign as listed above, with its planetary ruler alongside (so Aries, Mars; Taurus, Venus; and so on).
2. Next, alongside the planet, write the zodiac symbol (or draw it if you can). For Aries you would write 'ram', Taurus 'bull', Gemini 'twins', Cancer 'crab', and so on.
3. When you've finished this list, look at the words and symbols you've penned on each line and freely associate them with other words, ideas or qualities in your mind. You might look at 'Aries, Mars, ram' and then write down 'horns, pushy, red, fire, first sign of zodiac', and so on.
4. Do this for all 12 signs and see what words and ideas you come up with. Now check with the standard or traditional qualities associated with each sign and see if they match or have similarities. You can now begin to think in this symbolic way. This is one of the many simple keys to divination.

The solar pathway

When you were born, the sun was moving through a certain sign of the zodiac. This is known as your sun sign. But your sun sign isn't really representative of your personality as most people think; in fact, it's more an expression of your purpose, your life direction and what matters to you. Your personality may exhibit certain traits as an offshoot of that pathway, but the pathway is what you were born with and is the potential you have within you. This is your innate 'inspiration of the gods'. By divining your pathway you can then live your own future as you desire it to be. If you are already in accordance with the pathway chosen for you, then you're off to a good, positive start. If not, then perhaps it's time to do something about it?

Exercise: your pathway
What you will need:

> pen or pencil
> piece of A4 paper
> white candle

1. Whatever sun sign you are, draw a large circle on the piece of paper and place a large dot in the centre of it. Draw a horizontal line across the middle, crossing the dot, and a vertical line from top to bottom, crossing the dot. You have now quartered the circle.

2. In the first quarter, starting at the bottom left and working anticlockwise (this is how horoscopes work in astrology), draw or write what matters to you.

3. In the second quarter, at the bottom right, write or draw your deepest, most secret desire.

4. In the third quarter, top right, write any influences, whether external or in your mind (such as self-doubt or fear of the unknown), which are bothering you or which you believe are preventing you from doing what you most desire.

5. In the last quarter, top left, write what your pathway is (if you know it); if not, write what your mission in life is. If you still don't have one, think long and hard about what matters to you to help you discover your quest.

6. Take the paper and fold it twice, so that the quarters are folded together.

7. Put the white candle on top of the paper and light the candle. Sit for a few minutes concentrating on the candle flame, and first focus on what matters to you, then on your secret desire, then on what's blocking you, and finally, focus on your true pathway or mission.

8. Now look up the true potential of your sun sign in the next section, and see if it is in accord with what you have written. If it is, then obviously you are going to find it easier to make positive steps towards fulfilling those desires. If not, it's time to dig deeper into the real, inner you and discover what and who you truly are. Astrology can really help you.

The solar principle, and men and women

Men are often more in line with this solar principle of career direction, and you'll find them in careers or jobs that seem to be compatible with their sun sign. I hate to generalise, but women have, in the past, been more likely to express their pathway through personality traits, because, due to family or cultural expectations, they were not usually assigned a solar direction; for example, in many cultures, 'girl' equates with 'mother' with 'wife' and with 'housekeeper' (although this is obviously changing all the time). The solar principle is masculine; it defines a career person, the breadwinner, the solar core of the family or relationship, and for women, this vocational aspect of the sun often was blocked. We still carry this expectation in most cultures.

The sun

The sun is the most important part of your chart. It represents your core potential, motivation and inner drives. And that potential is one of the most significant things in astrology. It's there like a seed waiting to burst into life to become a flower or plant, but it's up to you what you do with that seed. And that means taking responsibility for your choices and yourself. Do you?

The sun also describes your sense of purpose and what matters to you, how you would like to be recognised and your sense of identity. Do you have one? If so, describe it to yourself now. With what or whom do you identify?

The exercise below will help you to identify with your quest too.

Exercise: my quest

What you will need:

pen or pencil
piece of A4 paper
seed
3 white quartz crystals

1. Draw a flower on the paper – any flower of your choice. Place the seed in the middle to represent your growing self.
2. Alongside or below the flower, write down the following statements, and once they've all been written down, finish off the lines one by one. If you write anything negative, ask yourself why, and start again until you are writing positive, self-loving words.

- I prefer friends and family to see me as

  _____

- I consider my lover or partner to be

  _____

- This seed represents what matters to me. That is

  _____

- I believe in my

  _____

- I identify with people who are

  _____

- I want to be

  _____

- My character is said to be

  _____

- This flower represents my gift of

  _____

3. Next, lay the three crystals in a line across the flower and say: 'From now on my potential will burst forth like a blossoming flower and I will follow my true pathway and what truly matters to me.'

4. Leave the paper with the three crystals for one lunar cycle to empower your words with universal energy.

5. Every time you doubt yourself, or question your quest, look at this piece of paper again and place the three crystals across the flower to maximise self-belief and follow your true pathway.

The cusp

The sun appears to move through each sign of the zodiac (the imaginary celestial belt and the path of the sun's ecliptic) throughout the year. It spends roughly one month in each sign. If you were born on the cusp, remember that you're either one sign or another – you can't be both! Being born on 'the cusp' means being born on the day that the sign moves from one zodiac sign to another; however, the sun changes signs at different times of day depending on the year, and sometimes the day itself changes too. So if you think you were born on the cusp, you need to check with a professional astrologer which sun sign you really are.

The four elements

According to the classical Greek philosopher Empedocles, the four elements were rather like building blocks or the pure components of the known universe. Later, Aristotle added a fifth element, which was called 'aether', also known as the quintessence, which became the secret ingredient in the practice of alchemy.

These days, only four elements are assigned to traditional Western astrology. The elements describe certain characteristics common to these following groups of signs in the zodiac:

The elements are: fire, earth, air and water.

In spell work, as we have seen, the elements also correspond to the four main points of the compass: fire – south, water – north, air – east, earth – west. By placing specific crystals in these areas of your home, you can enhance the symbolic power of each element's invisible energy and their qualities.

Three signs are allocated to each element.

- The **fire** signs are: Aries, Leo, Sagittarius
- The **earth** signs are: Taurus, Virgo, Capricorn
- The **air** signs are: Gemini, Libra, Aquarius
- The **water** signs are: Cancer, Scorpio, Pisces

Fire signs are: driven, feisty, self-motivated, idealistic, showy, competitive, challenging, flighty and physical

Earth signs are: organised, practical, productive, creative, devoted, nest-builders, constructive, reliable and sensual

Air signs are: unpredictable, paradoxical, light-hearted, romantic, carefree, laid-back, intellectual, astute, witty, wise and savvy

Water signs are: caring, artistic, spiritually aware, passionate, intuitive, emotional, dreamy, compassionate, sincere and instinctive

Exercise: get to know your element

Whatever sun sign you are, look up your element, if you don't know it already, and become totally immersed in that element's qualities for a whole day. This means being conscious of everything related to that element whether around you or through your actions; for example, if you're a Taurus, you're an earth sign, so you have to become earth itself for the day.

Here are some ideas to check into each element mode for the day.

BE EARTH FOR THE DAY
1. Adorn your body with jewels or pretty clothes.
2. Preen and pamper yourself; cook up an indulgent feast.
3. Declutter your wardrobe (earth people have to be uncluttered for success).

4. At work, speak gently but firmly, praise others for their talents, be organised and dedicated.
5. In love, be sensual, share chocolates, champagne or just a foaming bath.

BE FIRE FOR THE DAY

1. Show off your talents, exude confidence, get noticed.
2. Be glamour personified; flirt with a stranger or seduce your partner.
3. Go for a run or exercise outside.
4. Seize an opportunity to advance in work or love.
5. Take a risk on the lottery, book a weekend break away.

BE AIR FOR THE DAY

1. Start writing a novel; jot down notes for an amazing idea.
2. Seduce someone with your wit and words.
3. Phone all your pals, chat for hours, laugh in the rain.
4. Be a bit of a kid – play a board game or charades.
5. Do something unpredictable, but life enhancing.

BE WATER FOR THE DAY

1. Tell someone you care for them or love them.
2. Paint a portrait of yourself; listen to your favourite music.
3. Set up a sacred corner in your home for spell work.
4. Trust your intuition when making every decision.
5. Get back to nature, surround yourself with birdsong, or simply daydream.

The three qualities

As we have seen, another traditional way of dividing up the 12 signs is into three different groups of qualities. These are:

The cardinal signs: Aries, Cancer, Libra, Capricorn

These people are promoters. They are proactive, motivated, driven and ambitious. Cardinal signs instigate events and experiences; likewise each sign begins a season. In the northern hemisphere, therefore, Aries begins spring, Cancer begins summer, Libra begins autumn, and Capricorn begins winter.

The fixed signs: Taurus, Leo, Scorpio, Aquarius

These people are doers. They act out ideas and are stable, organised and focused; for example, if Aries has a grand idea about setting up an exciting business, Taurus will be the one who does all the leg work and can forge the idea into something viable.

The mutable signs: Gemini, Virgo, Sagittarius, Pisces

These signs are versatile, and willing to change and adapt to circumstances; for example, a Gemini would take the successful Taurus business and adapt and refine it to changing times or as fashion dictates. Mutable signs are chameleons but they aspire to perfection.

The houses

The other way the horoscope is divided up is into houses. There are many different systems for doing this, the most popular being the Placidus, Equal and Koch house systems. The house division is useful if you want to take a closer look at your own chart, because the houses define how and where the specific planetary angles and placements will show up in areas of your life; however, without a professionally drawn-up chart, it's not possible to determine in this book which planets fall into which houses. But it's useful to know what the houses are:

- 1st house – how I view the world; my sense of self
- 2nd house – my possessions, money, body, property and physical needs
- 3rd house – communication channels, trade, friends, short trips and travel
- 4th house – home, family, where I belong
- 5th house – creativity, children and love affairs
- 6th house – workplace, routines and well-being
- 7th house – relationships of all kinds
- 8th house – joint property, joint finances and sexuality
- 9th house – beliefs, journeys and education
- 10th house – career, public image, life direction
- 11th house – social life, groups of people and engaging in the world
- 12th house – spirituality, dreams and escapism

The houses are also ruled by various signs and elements; for example, the first house is assigned to Aries, fire and Mars, and so on round the zodiac.

Now it is time to see what life direction you might be wise to follow. Below is a brief introduction to your sun sign's potential life direction and a few ways your innate potential might be expressed through your personality.

Aries

Ruling planet: Mars
Symbol: the ram
Crystal: red carnelian

Your expression Irrepressible, impatient, fiery, driven, courageous, challenging, lusty, idealistic, insensitive

You like Freedom, competition, being in love, showing off, one-upmanship

You dislike Compromise, not getting your way, wimps, being told to wait for anything

Your pathway Make it clear to yourself that you know where you're going and, perhaps more importantly, why. Be number one and embrace a free, creative lifestyle where you can express your original ideas and goal-oriented spirit. You're always in one big hurry everywhere you go, beating others to the front of the queue, or you are the first to get to work. Hard-working and energetic, you're willing to take the risks that most people wouldn't dream of, and you are brilliant at reinventing new ways of doing traditional things, whether in politics or business.

Top vocations Head hunter, company director, barrister, solicitor, financial advisor, sports teacher, politician, art director, fire fighter, ambulance driver

Abracadabra Place a piece of red carnelian in the south area of your home to attract success your way.

Taurus
Ruling planet: Venus
Symbol: the bull
Crystal: emerald

Your expression Sensual, loyal, down-to-earth, reliable, vain, affectionate, possessive, jealous, determined, stable, creative

You like Feeling secure, being pampered, commitment, beautiful objects and people

You dislike Empty promises, being rushed, being told what to do, small portions of food

Your pathway As a true lover of luxury, beauty and money, you love to show off all your achievements. You're practical about finances and are suited to money-making careers such as banking, insurance and the stock exchange. With a fine eye for beauty and style, if you're not into finances, you'll be lavishing others with your gourmet skills or becoming some kind of creative guru.

Top vocations Investment banker, chef, artist, furniture designer/maker, musician, landscape gardener, interior designer, fashion designer, antique dealer, restaurant owner

Abracadabra To promote successful creative juices and shrewd investment, place two pieces of jade (for double power) in the west corner of your home.

Gemini
Ruling planet: Mercury
Symbol: the twins
Crystal: citrine

Your expression Mercurial, entertaining, talkative, witty, inconsistent, freedom loving, a game player, charming

You like Variety, discussing every subject under the sun, changing situations

You dislike Know-it-alls, possessiveness, routine, being bored

Your pathway You are best suited to working in an environment where you can create clever ideas. You are the ultimate punchy-message guru – such as caption writing, advertising, blogging and journalism. To flex your versatile mind, you're also suited to communicating information to the big wide world: translating ideas, illustrating books or ideas, or being a bit of a roadmap — informing people how to get from A to B by the shortest route or in the quickest time.

Top vocations Journalist, bookseller, advertising executive, courier, linguist, writer/author, tour guide, taxi driver, illustrator, news reader

Abracadabra Light a yellow candle and invoke the power of Mercury for inspiration and important contacts by saying: 'Communication is my talent, now lead me to where it proves me gallant.'

Cancer
Ruling planet: the moon
Symbol: the crab
Crystal: moonstone

Your expression Sensitive, sensual, nostalgic, subtle, introspective, moody, emotional, unpredictable, funny

You like Caring for others, your home, belonging to a group or clan, the past

You dislike People messing up your kitchen, taking risks, being bossed around

Your pathway If you're not rummaging around antique fairs or shopping for glamorous outfits, you'll surround yourself with nostalgic bits and bobs and fine works of art. Your sensitive and caring nature can be put to great use in an industry where your instinct for making people feel good about themselves can lead you to a key managerial or creative role. Money can sometimes buy you love, and you would make an excellent advisor in all financial institutions or working in a glamorous environment.

Top vocations Stock-market dealer, banker, hospital administrator, historian, archivist, counsellor, hotel manager, women's magazine editor, caterer, personnel officer

Abracadabra Write down the following as a list: waxing moon, full moon, waning moon, dark of the moon. Now look out for the changing phases on the Web or in an almanac. Write your true vocational desire beside each phase, then when you have completed one cycle, you can begin to manifest your vocation.

Leo
   Ruling planet: the sun
   Symbol: the lion
   Crystal: tiger's eye

Your expression Fiery, dramatic, vain, immature, romantic, stylish, flamboyant, demanding, self-centred, excessive

You like Glitzy accessories, a fan club, role-playing, exaggerated flattery, glamour

You dislike Routines, responsibilities, being ignored, rivals, reality

Your pathway You believe that you deserve the best because you believe you *are* the best at whatever you do. It's really important that you're on some sort of throne or stage surrounded by admirers. This will enable you to soar above the crowd, and look like you've made a million even if you haven't. The arts, film, theatre and the teaching professions will give you a medium for expressing your flair for drama or acting out a role.

Top vocations Celebrity, entertainer, exhibition organiser, film director/working in films, teacher, theatrical agent, educational advisor, obstetrician, creative director, singer

Abracadabra On a sunny day, take a piece of tiger's eye and push it into the earth of a potted sunflower or marigold, or bury it among some wild-flowering dandelions. Thank the sun for shining for you and soon the best things will come your way.

Virgo
Ruling planet: Mercury
Symbol: the Virgin
Crystal: peridot

Your expression Selective, dedicated, self-effacing, monogamous, sensual, intellectual, self-righteous, body-conscious

You like Clean linen, socks and a spotless bathroom, intelligent conversation, being pampered, honesty

You dislike Emotional scenes, ignorance, disorder, filthy fingernails

Your pathway It's said that you can edit anything, whether it's a politician's speech, an encyclopaedia, a film or someone else's laundry. With a natural talent for getting the message across, you iron out other people's mistakes with flair and sophistication. With such high standards, people in more powerful positions intuitively know that you will get the job done, researched and double-checked for flaws. Dedicated to health and fitness issues, you would also enjoy running your own health-food shop or gym.

Top vocations Literary agent, secretary, civil servant, computer programmer, copy editor, critic, dentist, dental hygienist, dietician, healer, fitness coach

Abracadabra The powder described here, when sprinkled around a circle, will seal your commitment to your flair for precision and dedication. Draw a large circle on paper. Sprinkle ground cinnamon around the circle. Write in the centre of the circle what you would like to dedicate yourself to, and leave the paper for one lunar cycle to activate your desire.

Libra

Ruling planet: Venus
Symbol: the scales
Crystal: sapphire

Your expression Seductive, indecisive, sophisticated, idealistic, subtle, rational, paradoxical, compliant, manipulative

You like Compliments, romantic conversations, beautiful people, socialising

You dislike Arguments, emotional scenes, loneliness, splitting up, disapproval

Your pathway With innate aesthetic talent, you can make a success in fashion, beauty, design or anything that is to do with taste. Beautifully packaged yourself, you create an atmosphere of perfection around you. This means that you need to work in a glamorous environment or a profession where you receive approval for your diplomatic skills. Run an art gallery, work behind the scenes in the theatre, slap make-up on film stars, or work at the local health spa or chic holiday resort where people love to have your sophisticated laid-back image around.

Top vocations Make-up artist, art dealer, wedding organiser, graphic designer, beauty therapist, interior designer, hairdresser, model, marriage counsellor, diplomat, lawyer

Abracadabra Find or draw an image of your ideal of beauty (whether male or female). Place a piece of white quartz crystal over it, and leave it in a secret place to promote glamour in your life.

Scorpio
Ruling planet: Pluto
Symbol: the scorpion
Crystal: obsidian

Your expression Erotic, passionate, extremist, stubborn, mysterious, manipulative, jealous, intense, compulsive

You like Everything erotic, money, power, intimacy, probing people's minds

You dislike Superficiality, niceties, gossiping, being told what to do

Your pathway A secret sense of invincibility means that you thrive in a profession where you can be at the top. You may not be out there on the stage; more likely, you'll be working behind the scenes, organising and controlling teams of people. Single-minded and passionate about everything you do, you may give up an ordinary lifestyle in your quest for power. You could even be drawn to industrial espionage where you can use your probing mind to uncover dark truths.

Top vocations Head hunter, industrial spy, film censor, criminologist, insurance investigator, tax collector/consultant, researcher, psychotherapist, pathologist, archaeologist

Abracadabra Take a piece of black obsidian and place it in the north corner of your home to attract to you the vocation you truly desire.

Sagittarius
Ruling planet: Jupiter
Symbol: the archer
Crystal: turquoise

Your expression Optimistic, adventurous, impulsive, extravagant, high spirited, freedom-loving, flashy, versatile.

You like Travelling, knowing all the best people, being seen in the best places, having fun

You dislike Making promises, possessive lovers, being serious about life

Your pathway Whether a great crusader or marketeer, you can persuade anyone to do anything as long as you keep busy and don't get bored. You excel at selling, buying, wheeling and dealing, and when taking a risk you usually fall on your feet. You can win new accounts or clinch a deal, because you're astute enough to be in the right place at the right time. Some people might call you lucky, but you're quick to learn who and what can lead you to that pot of gold.

Top vocations Explorer, travel writer, teacher/lecturer, sales or marketing person, travel agent, eternal student, horse trainer, airline pilot, publisher, philosopher

Abracadabra To help bring the right kind of opportunities your way, light three white candles and place a piece of turquoise in front of each. Say, 'With this light I will divine, all that must and will be mine.' Leave the candles to burn down, then keep the stones with you in all vocational situations to achieve results.

Capricorn
Ruling planet: Saturn
Symbol: the goat
Crystal: onyx

Your expression Self-sufficient, sensual, loyal, cautious, ambitious, highly sexed, traditional, insecure, critical, cool

You like Status, security, control, structure, maturity, classic fashion and ambitious people

You dislike Risks, the unknown, radical ideas, dreamers, laziness

Your pathway Even while living a normal family life, you still yearn for a position of great responsibility. You have an extraordinary instinct for how to climb the pecking order in either the establishment or glamour industry in your quest for power, the latter fuelled by an early sense of vulnerability. You can and will direct anything from films to restaurants or art galleries. And it is this sense of direction that gets you noticed and gives you the status you crave.

Top vocations Account executive, administrator, manager, property developer, government official, celebrity, film director, diamond expert, civil engineer, public speaker, geologist

Abracadabra Write your wish list on a piece of paper and fold or twist it around an onyx crystal. Place it under your bed and wait for amazing results in any career or vocational intention.

Aquarius

Ruling planet: Uranus
Symbol: the water bearer
Crystal: amber

Your expression Quirky, aloof, avant-garde, independent, intellectual, glamorous, truthful, idealistic

You like Personal freedom, humanitarian and animal rights, intelligence, minimalist or a green lifestyle, talking about everything in the universe

You dislike Emotions, marriage, possessiveness, weepy films, conventional expectations

Your pathway Forward-thinking and progressive, you would make an excellent research scientist, educator or fashion guru. Intuitively, you tap into future trends, and can tailor your professional lifestyle to suit whatever's going to be the flavour of the month. With an eye for the unconventional and also for humanitarian issues, you would find great joy in crusading for animal and human welfare, or upsetting the political applecart with your brave new global ideology.

Top vocations Scientist, hi-tech whizz-kid, dealer in futures, humanitarian reformer, fashion designer/trendsetter, educational advisor, psychologist, ecologist, inventor, astrologer

Abracadabra Sprinkle some basil leaves or dried basil in your shoes, and wherever you go you will be loved for your ideas and for who you are. This will bring you contacts who can help you to succeed.

Pisces

Ruling planet: Neptune
Symbol: the fish
Crystal: amethyst

Your expression Mystical, easily hurt, dreamy, impressionable, dependent, beautiful, romantic, escapist, elusive

You like Music, art, candlelit dinners, acting, evasion, romance, dreaming

You dislike Direct confrontation, making decisions, reality

Your pathway Loving harmony and a laid-back environment makes it hard for you to find a workplace where you can relax, but if you're truly happy to work with and care for others, then the healing and spiritual professions will suit you best. With such a powerful imagination, the alternative Pisces vocation is to express your innate talent for art, music, acting or writing.

Top vocations Musician, photographer, writer, vet, actress, working with animals, psychic healer, secret agent, social worker, artist

Abracadabra On the night of a new moon, write down your greatest wish. Take an amethyst crystal, partly dipped in rose oil, and stamp the oily part over the wish. Leave the crystal until the full moon for your wish to come true.

The other planets in your horoscope

Your personal horoscope, more commonly known as the birth chart, is unique to you, depending on the time, date and place of your birth. The patterns, angles and positions of the planets and their emphasis in elements or the houses completes the total picture of that moment in time when you were born. Some people express these potentials through certain expressions of their personality (which are dependent on prominent planets or signs), vocation (as with the sun) or relationships (Venus, the moon and the other planets). Let's now look at what each planet represents in your chart and how it can manifest in your life.

The moon sign

The moon's placement determines your feelings, emotions, moods, reactions, needs, sense of home, belonging and instincts for caring and nurturing:

- When the moon is in the **fire** signs, you need excitement, adventure, action, to be centre stage, passion.
- When the moon is in the **earth** signs, you need security, comfort, stability, to be in control, traditional value.
- When the moon is in the **air** signs, you need to communicate, to have light-hearted fun, to play, to analyse, to have an unconventional lifestyle.

- When the moon is in the **water** signs, you need to be needed, to have emotional empathy, compassion, to give, to care, to express feelings through talent, to belong.

But what if your sun sign is not the same as your moon sign? For example, if you have the moon in the fire signs, you may *need* (moon) rather than *desire* (sun) a lot of passion and excitement in your life. (The sun affects what matters to you or gives you a sense of purpose.) Let's take this example a bit further. If you had the sun in Taurus (earth) and the moon in Aries (fire), you might find that there's a conflict between your solar Taurus desire for a down-to-earth, secure vocation and your fiery lunar need for risk-taking. Get it?

Mercury
This fast-moving planet describes how we communicate, how we use our mind, make connections and transmit information, and our ability to rationalise or use logic:

- When Mercury is in the **fire** signs, you might communicate quickly, talk before thinking through, be astute but rash and outspoken.
- When Mercury is in the **earth** signs, you might be thoughtful, opinionated, taciturn, tactful, discrete, analytical and eloquent.
- When Mercury is in the **air** signs, you might be analytical, rational, quick-witted, amusing, flippant, also (paradoxically) contradictory and adaptable.

- When Mercury is in the **water** signs, you might be poetic, dreamy, erratic, scattered, illogical, intense, unfocused, discrete.

Venus

Our pleasure principle is Venus's territory. The planet's placement describes how we love, and how we give and receive pleasure, also our values in love and towards money and possessions, and how we share, cooperate and relate on a loving level:

- When Venus is in the **fire** signs, you love passionately, expect all or nothing in love, and look for adventurous love; you can be spontaneous, feisty, unpredictable, idealistic and optimistic.
- When Venus is in the **earth** signs, you can be sensual and indulgent, have strong materialistic values, prefer conventional relating, be realistic and companionable.
- When Venus is in the **air** signs, you love light-hearted romance, fall for a pretty face, you can be idealistic, unreliable, fun-loving and inspiring.
- When Venus is in the **water** signs, you might be bewitching, romantic, elusive, falling in love with love, and have unrealistic expectations; you love to merge, and a spiritual connection is important to you.

Mars

Mars describes the way in which we go out and get what we want. The planet reveals how we assert our desires, courage, competitive urge, physical lust and sexual libido:

- When Mars is in the **fire** signs, you might be pushy, potent, impulsive, blunt, arrogant, sexually alert, challenging and dramatic about getting your way.
- When Mars is in the **earth** signs, you might be dominant, demanding, controlling, with a strong ego, consistent, dogmatic and organised about getting what you want.
- When Mars is in the **air** signs, you might be restless, inconsistent, hasty, indecisive and changeable, and you might analyse the situation before going for gold.
- When Mars is in the **water** signs, you might be cautious, secretly competitive and inclined to use manipulative tactics to get what you want.

Jupiter

Jupiter inflates your desires, describes your beliefs, your philosophy, where you're greedy, and also what you are best at achieving (not necessarily vocational) or where you are naturally talented:

- When Jupiter is in the **fire** signs, you might be crusading, campaigning and physically passionate, with exaggerated beliefs, despotic and best at crusading for a cause, selling and leading the pack.

- When Jupiter is in the **earth** signs, you might be the ultimate gourmet, a lover of all the pleasures of the flesh; you're best when being creative.
- When Jupiter is in the **air** signs, you can be the ultimate diplomat, prosaic, preachy, a bit of a know-it-all, exaggerating the truth but never lying. You're best at ruling the world!
- When Jupiter is in the **water** signs, you might have an exaggerated desire to find a spiritual belief system; you tend to confuse romance with love and want to merge. You are at your best in music and the performing arts.

Saturn

This planet is known for its association with authority, convention and discipline. But it also describes where we feel we are most clumsy in life and how, ironically, in later life, we become masters of the very thing we found so awkward when young. It also represents our Achilles heel – where we feel most vulnerable and how we psychologically defend ourselves:

- When Saturn is in the **fire** signs, when young we can be uncomfortable about our ego, desires and self-esteem. Later, we compensate by masterfully playing the self-centred, motivated star of the show or develop the 'I can do it better than you' syndrome.

- When Saturn is in the **earth** signs, when young we might be impractical, lacking self-worth, finding that reality is a chore, and being clumsy with possessions. Later, we can develop powerful creativity and a sense of order, and we might become an effective entrepreneur or material achiever. We might compensate through empire building.

- When Saturn is in the **air** signs, when young we might find it hard to relate, communicate, listen and learn. Later, we might perfect the art of compromise. We can compensate by becoming the ideal partner, but if too willing to please, we resent everyone else.

- When Saturn is in the **water** signs, when we are young we might be lost in a fog or a confused atmosphere, struggling to create an identity. Later, we might develop a powerful aura around the self; the good news is that this can lead to a highly creative life, or being so in control of oneself that one becomes ruthless.

The outer planets

These three planets take a long time to move through the signs, so they are more concerned with generational influences; however, where they contact a personal planet in our chart, their influence becomes a lifelong curse or a talent, depending on the planet, the angles and so on. Check with a professional astrologer to work with these.

Uranus The urge to rebel, freedom, independence, sudden awakening, revolutionary change, radical ideas and reformation of the norm. Sexual electricity.

Neptune Purification, deception, illusions, romantic idealisation, escapism, sacrifice, enchantment. Dissolving boundaries. Seduction.

Pluto Transformation, obsessive desires, compulsive power, violation, the dark side of love. Plummeting to the depths; the taboo and the sacred.

Relationships and getting on

Traditionally, the three signs of each element tend to harmonise with one another – apart from the odd hiccup. Getting along with the other elements is a little more challenging, but in fact this can be a big attraction. For what we may believe we lack in ourselves, we often find delightfully refreshing in another person, and in that way we import those missing qualities into our lives.

Fire – firing on all cylinders Aries gets excited about adventurous holidays, Sagittarius will be happy to go on impulse, whereas Leo will want to organise and add luxury touches to the whole event to ensure that they are stars of the holiday show! Two fire signs make for passionate partners, but they can find it hard to make compromises.

Air – airy fairies Gemini will be fascinated with Libra's cool head and graceful ways, Libra will enjoy the light-hearted spirit of Gemini, and Aquarius can relate to both because there's no pressure to renounce their own free spirit. These can be intellectually stimulating combinations, but two airheads can make for a highly impractical lifestyle.

Earth – down to earth The love of stability and routine, coupled with a hefty dose of common sense, make all these three sensible couples. Taurus enjoys Capricorn's ambitious streak, and Capricorn knows he or she can rely on Taurus to follow through, whereas Virgo loves to clean up after either; however, all three can feel the partnership lacks a light-hearted spirit of adventure, unless one or other has a gang of planets in the air or fire signs.

Water – water babes Cancer cares, Scorpio probes the emotional depths and Pisces merges into whatever soulmate the other is seeking. These pairings are highly romanticised and mutually sensitive together, but emotionally they can all get sucked into melodramatics and escapist dramas by having to deal with so many whirlpools of feeling.

Mutually supportive combinations
Fire and air The fire signs are traditionally said to get on quite well with air. Air fans the fire signs' flames and adapts to their blazing qualities. Meanwhile, fire adores air's versatile nature and spontaneity.

The **earth** signs traditionally get on with **water**, as the practical earth person likes the support of empathetic water. Water loves to have someone around to do all those things that they just don't have the energy to do!

Difficult energies

Signs which are traditionally less compatible are fire with water, and air with earth:

Fire and water A very simple analogy is that water puts out fire's flames. The water person can dampen fire's enthusiasm and *joie de vivre* under their own foggy emotions. On the other side, fire is often too impulsive and carefree for water's sensitive nature.

Earth and air Air signs need space; they don't like being controlled nor do they have a thing about assets, materialism or security. Air finds earth signs bring them down to earth with a huge bump, but eventually they may get bored with the practicalities of life. Earth is fascinated by air's light-hearted approach to life but needs a serious partner, not just pretty words.

Cycles and returns

Astrology is a fabulous tapestry in itself, because it includes a tangled web of cycles, harmonies and everything you could want from the greatest orchestra in the sky, which was once known by the ancients as 'the music of the spheres'.

As these cycles change and shift around the zodiac, they can be seen to highlight angles and planets in our own chart; for example:

If you have Venus in Cancer for example, and Venus aligns to a full moon, this energy would remind you of your own depth of feeling.

When the sun and Mars are aligned, this resonates with someone who has the sun in Aries (Aries is ruled by Mars), reminding them that they are a force to be reckoned with.

Saturn takes a long time to get once round the zodiac (about 30 years), so when it aligns with your own Saturn there's a tremendous shift in your outlook in life. (See below.)

As these cycles weave and change, we can look at a few of them in relation to our own chart. Apart from the more well-known cycles of the sun and moon there are the cycles of Mercury, Venus, Mars, Saturn and Jupiter. The outer planets (Neptune, Uranus and Pluto) move so slowly that they have long-term generational consequences, which we won't worry about in this little book.

Solar cycle The sun takes twelve months to whizz around the zodiac, and each time it returns to within a few degrees of the place it was when we were born.

Lunar cycles Because the moon moves quickly, it takes about four weeks to move around the zodiac. It is also, like the sun, able to be seen – although most of the time at night. This is when we see it changing from a new crescent moon, waxing or growing towards a full moon, then gradually waning back to a tiny crescent again until it disappears from view. It's easy to work with the four major phases of its cycle, as revealed in the spells section in Chapter 3.

People born under the dark of a new moon (in other words, you can't see the new moon at all) are thought to be discreet and secretive. Those born during a crescent waxing moon are creative types.

Those born under a full moon are emotionally driven to succeed, whereas those born under a waning crescent moon are self-reliant, self-contained, and less upfront.

Mercury cycles are inconsistent, ebbing and flowing, but tending to keep up with the solar year cycle. First they are fast, then slow, then retrograde (see page 208) then they move forward again and so on. It is a little tricky to keep track of Mercury unless you regularly consult an ephemeris (an astronomical diary).

Venus and Mars are also quite speedy, and although Mars gets round the zodiac in two years and Venus in one, like Mercury they are both erratic because of their back-tracking (retrograde) motion.

However, the cycles of Jupiter and Saturn are useful to know about as they are good marker points for longer periods of our life. These are known as the two major returns of Jupiter and Saturn.

Returns

Jupiter's return Jupiter takes about 12 years to complete one circuit of the zodiac, so every 12 or so years of your life, you will get a 'Jupiter return'. In other words, when you're about 12, 24, 36, 48, and so on, Jupiter returns to the place where it was when you were born and can trigger events, experiences which signal something about yourself, or push home to you what Jupiter really means in your chart.

Jupiter's influence inflates and amplifies characteristics and experiences in life, so take a look back at what experiences might be repeat themes in your life at those ages. You might find these magical periods of your life will enlighten you to the next Jupiter return and how you can go about making use of the qualities associated with Jupiter in your sign.

Saturn return Saturn's slower orbit around the horoscope (about 30 years for one cycle) enables us to grow into our Saturn selves. In other words, we become more able to deal with the very thing we feel we are clumsy at being with every turn of the time-lord's clock. Therefore, at the age of 30-ish, my analogy is that this is a great time to give birth. The midwife says, 'Go on push dear, push!' You struggle to push and it's the most painful experience you've ever had, and then suddenly it's all over and you're handed a nice cup of tea. And the midwife says, 'Didn't you do well?' Of course, then you're suddenly confronted with the responsibility of a newborn infant – and yes, it's a human being, you are no longer alone! Arggh! Responsibility! This Saturn return at 30, then, is when you have to start to realise that you are like the first-time mother, suddenly not alone, you have duties, a time to reap what you have sown, a time to accept what you have had growing in you for all those 30 years, the awkwardness you so long have neglected or avoided. Now it stares you in the face and you must deal with it.

What better way than turning an apparent failing into a super-refined grace? Let's take an example: a woman with Saturn in Libra. She's spent most of her relationship life up until the age of 30 not really knowing how to relate. She compromises, doesn't stick up for herself and adapts too easily, not realising that relating is about equality; she feels uncomfortable sharing anything. She'd rather do her own thing. She swings between the heady Libran delights of romance and idealising a partner, then once she's got it, she can't deal with the reality. At 30 she begins to realise that she could actually become quite good at this relating lark, because she's had so much practice. She appears so independent, and she seduces well, loves to please, shows how loving she can be, and becomes during the rest of her life the perfect lover, wife, romantic and crusader for beauty and truth. Venusian symmetry (Libra's ruler is Venus), both in art, life and love, truly becomes her passport to success. But deep down she hates all this relationship stuff and yearns for her independence. Yet she acquires the very skill that she found so awkward or was fearful of at a younger age.

For more information about Saturn returns in your chart, you are welcome to get in touch with me direct on my website (see page i).

Retrograde planets

What does it mean when we say 'Mercury's retrograde'? Oh, we do go on about it, us astrologers. But yes, what we mean is that this is a period when computers will crash, papers will be lost, phones won't work, text messages will be unwritten, travel will be held up, and so on.

What is a retrograde planet then? Put simply, it's the apparent movement of a planet moving backwards or, in the jargon, going retrograde through the zodiac. This apparent backtracking is symbolic of a time for more reflection, less energy expended on doing things and concentrating on all actions beginning with 're': renovation, rejuvenation, research, refocus, restore, re-invent, and so on – and I'm sure you can think of some suitable ones for your own personal retro times.

If you think about it, only 30 years ago or so before the invention of mobile phones, communication moved at a slower pace. If a letter took three days to reach someone, no one panicked. Lovers ran down to the letterbox in the vain hope that their beloved had managed to put pen to paper in the last week, or even month, but then for the rest of the day they forgot about it until the next day. In my youth, we may have sat waiting by the home phone hoping it would ring, or leave it off the hook when we went out to grab a gin and tonic, but we didn't run our lives around every second we didn't get a text message. Mercury retrograde in those days didn't slow down the letter writing, but gave the beloved a chance to get the words in the right order and to retire, retreat and review the situation before making assumptions.

It's actually beneficial, rather than a curse, when Mercury is retrograde. It may upset our fast-paced, hi-tech lifestyle, but it also puts us back on track. It reminds us that life isn't just about having it all now. It may actually slow us down to give us a chance to rethink what we really want from love and life.

Eclipses

I wrote a short poem once, which sums up the time from a solar eclipse to a lunar eclipse:

> *An eclipse, they cry? Oh, woe betide!*
> *When kings and courtiers run and hide.*
> *But what has been comes back full circle,*
> *To blot out that which cannot serve us,*
> *Until the full moon's own demise,*
> *When earth's great shadow spills the lies.*

In other words – if you're not into poetry – a solar eclipse is when the past (the moon) blots out the future (the sun) and we need to look at things in the past that are not resolved or could still be relevant to us now. A lunar eclipse is when the present (the earth) blots out the past (the moon), and current affairs and present thoughts for the future become more important than those from the past. You see how these cycles interact? They teach us that we should at times concentrate on the present/future, then the past, then again the present/future.

Reading a birth chart

This takes a lot of skill and astrological know-how, so get in touch with a professional qualified astrologer, or attend some classes at somewhere like the Faculty of Astrological Studies in London to learn your stuff properly. Of course, you can get a computer print-out of your chart and find some great books these days that describe all the different planetary placements and aspects, and what these all mean, but putting it all together is the hard part and it does take work and objective interpretation.

Start with the basics, and grow slowly but surely into your true potential. Astrology takes years to study, but that studying never stops. In fact, astrology is a life-time quest, and one that each of us can enjoy as we discover more and more about ourselves each day.

From the study of the sun, moon and planets, where you've learnt to pin-point a little more about the magic of who you are and where you are going in life, let's move on to tarot, palmistry and numerology. These are three of the most popular ways to 'read' the future or, rather, make decisions to take control of how you want your future to be, and how to live your life.

Chapter 6

Using the Tarot, Palmistry and Numerology

Traditionally, tarot, palmistry and numerology are among the most popular ways to divine the future, to know the truth about the past and to live well in the present. In this chapter you'll discover the basics of each of these methods, and discover more about your own magical self, too.

The tarot

All divination is positive if you have a positive attitude. Divination, as we have seen, is about seeing the past, present and future all as one, but also knowing that you are responsible for the choices you make at any given moment.

The tarot is a mirror of our true selves *at any given moment* and can give us insight into how to make choices for future benefits.

The tarot as a mirror

The 78-card tarot deck is made up of a series of images, which we all, strangely enough, seem to understand on a certain level. The psychologist, Carl G Jung, called these images 'archetypal' images. In the most basic terms an archetype is a blueprint, or a basic quality, experience, emotion or feeling that is common to us all. When we see the card called The Lovers, for example, we know this is about love and romance, or sexual chemistry. If we see the card called The Sun, most of us will see that this represents joy, happiness, and so on.

In fact, the tarot *mirrors* all facets of you and reflects your psyche (your soul-self at the deepest level) at any given moment of time. These reflections of ourselves have been seen by people over thousands and thousands of years in other kinds of mirrors too. These may be looking glasses from the real and man-made world – whether Egyptian or medieval hand mirrors, window glass – or via reflections of ourselves in water, crystal or ice. When we gaze at our mirror image, we see in the mirror an inverted reflection of ourselves, but whether it is the truth of who we are, or not, is where the tarot comes in.

When you look in a normal mirror (do it now, if you have one to hand) you recognise something, don't you? Yourself. Your face, nose and so on – the 'you' you've been seeing for years and years. Whether you like what you see or not is another matter, and therefore we tend to qualify that reflection with, 'Hmm, I could do with a visit to the hairdresser' or, 'I've got a line! Eek! Out with the wrinkle cream!' The tarot, on the other hand, reflects only the truth of who we are at any moment in time.

Projection and the tarot

In the same way that we can throw negative and positive vibes at our reflected image, so we can project our feelings on to the tarot too.

When you look at these mirrored images of the deepest part of your soul, there will be some that you may like, such as The World representing being at one with life, or The Emperor for protection. Others you may loathe, such as Death, representing a big change, or the Tower of Destruction for pointing to things suddenly falling apart. This is because you are projecting your personal feeling on to the tarot as you would project your current likes and dislikes on the mirror image of yourself; however, conversely, some of us might like the idea of change (Death) and hate the idea of being at one with anything (The World). Get it?

Always remember that with the tarot what you see is what you get, and the tarot never lies.

A brief history

Although the tarot as we know it today evolved from Italian playing cards of the 14th century, decks of mystical numbered cards existed as far back as ancient Egypt and Chinese Taoist cultures. These older decks may have been brought to Europe by travellers, traders and crusaders in the medieval period, and they soon became associated with fortune-telling in 16th-century Europe.

The 18th-century French occultist Antoine Court de

Gébelin, believed the tarot originated from an ancient Egyptian set of mystical tablets used by priests and magi to discover the secrets of the universe.

I like this identification, it adds mystery to the tarot, which, to be honest, when you start to use it, is exactly that: mysteriously revealing.

By the end of the 19th century, with the widespread interest in the occult, magic and divination, the mystic scholar Arthur Edward Waite, and his colleague the artist Pamela Colman Smith, developed their own set of tarot, now known as the ever-popular Rider-Waite deck. This is the favoured deck to use these days because all the suit cards are pictorial.

Getting to know the tarot

The deck of 78 cards is made up of 22 Major Arcana cards, and 56 cards divided into four suits known as the Minor Arcana. The word 'arcana' derives from a Latin word, meaning 'secrets'.

The Major Arcana are a series of archetypal images that resonate to the deepest part of our collective world soul and personal soul. They are like stepping stones to a personal story of psychological or spiritual enlightenment. Starting with The Fool (the unnumbered card) who first leaps off to innocently begin life's adventure, to the last card, The World, where he comes full circle to know himself. The Fool also represents you, as you embark on your tarot journey.

Choosing your deck

There is a wide range of decks available, but to start with I recommend the Rider-Waite deck, or the Universal Tarot, which is based on Rider-Waite. Both include specific images for each of the pip cards. Pip cards are the numbered cards, one to ten in a pack of cards. In playing-card decks you have five diamond symbols on the five-of-diamonds card, or three club symbols on the three-of-clubs card. (In some tarot decks you also get pip cards without any imagery, and these can be difficult to get your head around when first starting out. So decks which have a different image for every numbered or pip card are much easier to interpret.)

How to work with the tarot

Magic is about believing you can make something happen, and so when we are in harmony with the universal energy that pervades all, we can tap into the truth of the moment to achieve stuff or develop our talents for future happiness. The tarot links us to that universal truth when we shuffle the cards randomly, and is the interconnection between divine knowledge and future outcome. In fact, based on that moment you will be acting from that knowledge.

The key, the door, the truth

I always use this three-step metaphor for learning and interpreting the tarot. If you feel lost when confronted with a card, use these three words like a mantra in your head, and you'll soon be an expert yourself.

THE KEY – DO NOT JUDGE OR PROJECT

The key to working with the tarot is not to judge or project your fears, negative thoughts or even expectations on to any card you pick; for example, 'Oh, it's that evil-looking Devil card,' or 'The Emperor reminds me of my cruel tyrant of a partner.' Conversely, you may pick The World and imagine the best, 'I am going to be as grand as the world itself!' This is just as dangerous, because you may be identifying with pompous conceit.

Once you remember the key, and trust in the true interpretation of the card and your intuition, you can then open the tarot door.

THE DOOR – OPEN WITH HONESTY

In every image there are symbols that hold simple but deep truths. Some you may connect with, others you may not understand. The tarot holds all the secrets of the universe in its 78 cards. Each card is a doorway between our conscious world and the universal storehouse of knowledge. It is a portal to everything you want to know or desire to happen. In other words, the tarot is a door to a magical life. The door means: 'what you see is what you get'.

THE TRUTH ROOM

The truth is hidden in the tarot image you see before you. Once you are inside the truth room and begin to interpret the card, you will discover how the cards are helping to reveal what you really desire, or what matters to you. You have then passed through that magical doorway to face your own truth room, and you can begin to activate or manifest those truths into your life.

Shuffling the cards

People have different ways of shuffling cards, and as tarot cards are a lot bigger than normal playing cards, and there are a lot more of them, it's understandable that it can seem a bit of an effort. I've seen even professional tarot-card readers struggling with the oversized deck.

The simplest way is to spread them out face down on a table or on the floor in a long line, and then pick up a few at a time from different parts of the line and shuffle the two parts together as you would normal cards, and then place them in a pile to the left or right of the line. Continue doing this with several sections of cards until you have a nice pile, and then cut them three times. (Three is the ancient magic number for connecting to the universe.) The more you can shuffle, the more you are letting go of your personal power and letting the universal energy synchronise with your cards.

Concentrate

As you shuffle, concentrate on the issue or question to which you want to know the answer. There's not much point in thinking, *Oh well, I won't ask anything, I'll just see what turns up.* That's a statement about your current attitude to life. It's like saying, 'Oh well, I won't make any effort or make decisions about what I want for the future and just leave it to fate and chance.' Basically, doing that is, in a way, saying you have no future. What you put out to the universe (even if it's said unconsciously) is usually what you get back. In this case, it would be nothing.

If you don't believe in your future being something you can forge to the best of your ability and reap positive rewards, you won't. If you believe, you will, and I mean *truly* believe you will, then you will.

Think about what you desire, feel and believe what matters to you right now as you choose the cards, whether it's a new relationship, getting an old one revitalised, a new job or taking a risk, or going off in a completely different direction.

Laying the cards out

Now you've got to choose each card and lay them out in a spread. For this, place the deck face down on the table after you've cut it, and now make a long line of overlapping cards to the left or right (as you did when shuffling). Keep focusing on your question, and when you feel ready, run your finger slowly along the line back and forth, and stop when you sense a card is the right one or is even prompting you to pick it.

Depending on which layout you choose to do (see page 238), lay the cards in the appropriate placements before beginning to interpret them.

Card for the day

Before you do any of the spreads suggested in this book, it's a great idea to take one card for the day or evening ahead. This is one of the quickest ways to begin to learn to interpret the cards.

1. Start with just the 22 Major Arcana as these are the cards that best mirror what's going on for you right now.
2. Shuffle the cards, either as suggested before, or by shuffling in your hands – it's a lot easier with only 22 – then cut them three times.
3. Spread them out on the table or floor in a line, or an easier way when choosing only one card is to hold the deck in one hand and flick through them slowly with the other hand, until a card feels or seems right to choose. As you do so, concentrate on the day or evening ahead, and ask what events will manifest during this time.
4. Later in the day, you can look back and decide how the card manifested in your life during the day. Perhaps your initial interpretation wasn't what you expected, but perhaps it was relevant in a way that you *hadn't expected*? This is why it's always important to learn to relate cards to the questions you ask and to check the interpretation rather than jumping to conclusions. Some people are spooked by The Tower card, for example, but The Tower is simply about expecting the unexpected. Eventually, you will intuitively know what the card means without having to look it up.

The Major Arcana

Here are the 22 Major Arcana Cards, with their crystal and astrological associations. I have added some brief keyword and phrase interpretations for general and love spreads, and I've also included a short oracle to help you adapt the straightforward interpretations into a different sense or quality for the card:

The Fool
Unnumbered
Crystal: orange carnelian
Astro link: Uranus

General keywords Ignorance is bliss; blind to the truth; rushing to get somewhere without forethought. Adventurous but irresponsible; carefree but careless; enthusiastic and optimistic.

Love keywords Falling in love too quickly; immature attitude; impulsive or infatuated.

Oracle Life is the air you breathe and romance like the passion in your heart. Be self-reliant no matter how challenging the beginning.

The Magician
Arcanum 1
Crystal: topaz
Astro link: Mercury

General keywords Confidence, persuasive power and adapting to change are the route forward. Taking the initiative; sorting out your ideas; being inspirational; communicating effectively.

Love keywords Being romantically flexible; making a key love choice; showing you mean what you say.

Oracle Use your skill to create a new enterprise, stick to what you know. Avoid idealistic expectations, as making the right choice is now your best bet.

The High Priestess
Arcanum 2
Crystal: Opal
Astro link: the moon

General keywords Secrets revealed; trusting in your intuition; resorting to feminine wiles or subtle powers; someone else revealing a secret to you.

Love keywords Being able to seduce; you and a lover/ partner have a telepathic connection; you will be enlightened about a love secret; hidden feelings; sub-rosa or clandestine affair.

Oracle Mystery lies within our hearts as well as in the souls of others. Seek first to discover your own enigma of love before trying to reveal that of someone else.

The Empress
Arcanum 3
Crystal: green tourmaline
Astro link: Venus

General keywords Progress, determined feminine power or disruptive female influence; creative goals and action bring rewards; sensual pleasure and material interests are important.

Love keywords Strong feelings; a creative bond; sensual indulgence and physical desire. A need to mother your lover or partner – but don't smother.

Oracle Trust in your own whispers, not those of your thoughts but those of feelings. Listen to the wind and the earth; keep close to the ground.

The Emperor
Arcanum 4
Crystal: red carnelian
Astro link: Aries

General keywords Authority or powerful influences; a father figure causing problems; tactless and insensitive contacts; being assertive; taking the helm or leading a team.

Love keywords Attraction to a father figure or strong character; a cold-hearted or power-tripping lover; not being able to trust a lover's true intentions.

Oracle Confidence fires respect and effect, but your thoughts must complement your actions.

The Hierophant
   Arcanum 5
   Crystal: rose quartz
   Astro link: Taurus

General keywords Spiritual advisor, guru or professional mentor who comes into your life; trusting in traditional or conventional ways; unwillingness to adapt; clinging to the past.

Love keywords Meeting someone you feel you've known before; not accepting a change in a relationship; forming a romantic connection with a mentor, teacher or advisor.

Oracle Hold on to your beliefs in life, but always be open to new opinions. Unfurl your ideas carefully and learn understanding.

The Lovers
   Arcanum 6
   Crystal: citrine
   Astro link: Gemini

General keywords Making a choice; having to commit yourself before you want to; your heart rules your head; the power of love and how to deal with it; temptation and conflict of interests if you aren't decisive.

Love keywords New romance; physical desire can be fulfilled; a love triangle will test the strength of an existing relationship; having to choose between two people; what does love mean to you?

Oracle Love is sometimes like driving into a blizzard. You are snow blind, there is silence, but you still move on. Listen to your intuition to show you the way.

The Chariot
Arcanum 7
Crystal: moonstone
Astro link: Cancer

General keywords Being pulled in two directions and unsure of which to take; being realistic, persevering; taking hold of the reins of your life and achieving success; will power needed now.

Love keywords Getting your way and standing up for what you believe about a love affair, re-evaluating a relationship to ensure its success; taking control of the love chariot.

Oracle In a rush for cover, emotions run deep, and so does a desire to escape the truth. But discover your own powers of self-control and take the reins of destiny in your hands.

Strength

Arcanum 8
Crystal: tiger's eye
Astro link: Leo

General keywords Taking control of your life; being courageous and determined; self-empowerment brings you results; facing up to reality; future power struggle is indicated, but you will win.

Love keywords Are you giving too much of yourself, or expecting too much from love or a partner? Equally, are you trying too hard to control the relationship, or are they? Self-awareness will bring you joy.

Oracle Your heart is as courageous as your instinct to move on. Liberate your anger, feel strong, and welcome the power of giving and receiving.

The Hermit

Arcanum 9
Crystal: peridot
Astro link: Virgo

General keywords reflection and discrimination are needed when making a choice; facing up to the truth; looking within; use discretion and tact in any business dealings.

Love keywords Looking back with regret about a past love affair won't make a current one better; think long and hard before committing yourself; reflect before revealing your feelings.

Oracle Secrets guarded beneath the wings of fear can be freed with generous hearts. Discovery is about self, and love is about discovery.

The Wheel of Fortune
Arcanum 10
Crystal: lapis lazuli
Astro link: Jupiter

General keywords *Carpe diem* – seize the day; opportunity awaits you; a new cycle in your life is beginning, an old one ending; don't fear change – embrace it.

Love keywords Drop emotional baggage and move on; a new romance or infatuation is coming your way; unexpected events will change your love life for the better; the timing is right for personal happiness.

Oracle Seekers search their wheels for answers. They look back or forward but never gaze at the present moment. Time is the invention of man, but love is timeless, unwatched, unhurried. It is destiny, it is this moment – the moment is now.

Justice
Arcanum 11

Crystal: Jade
Astro link: Libra

General keywords time to make a decision; being fair and objective; balance and poise; legal issues will have a positive outcome; listen to others' advice and communicate the truth.

Love keywords Clarity needed about equality in a relationship; all is fair in love and war; decide how to make a new romance work out; are you willing to compromise or are you stubborn about your desires?

Oracle Love curves its way through life, permeating all. It is not angular, not simply straight arrows to the heart but often arrives on a gusty wind of chance.

The Hanged Man
Arcanum 12
Crystal: blue lace agate
Astro link: Neptune

General keywords A time for transition or readjusting your beliefs; looking at life from a different perspective. Are you at a crossroads? Time to get out of a rut; feeling in limbo.

Love keywords Transform a static or dull relationship – don't make sacrifices for others; free yourself from someone's manipulative tactics; think carefully about what you want from the future.

Oracle For one moment, hesitate. Take a step back, look again at what you have, and surrender yourself to the truth.

Death
Arcanum 13
Crystal: malachite
Astro link: Scorpio

General keywords Don't take this card literally, please. This card always signifies some kind of change, new beginning and the end of a cycle and the beginning of a new one. It could be a life direction, a new pathway, career change or a belief system.

Love keywords Letting go of old values and changing your love life for the better; if single, an imminent new romance; if attached, a change that heralds renewed vitality, or a brilliant partnership.

Oracle Drop past baggage, restrict emotions, relinquish decayed love. Love is a journey not a destination.

Temperance
Arcanum 14
Crystal: turquoise
Astro link: Sagittarius

General keywords Compromise or agree to differ; moderation in all things is the key to success; harmonious dealings; self-control; blending of ideas; clarification of aspirations.

Love keywords Harmony between your desires and your needs; balanced relating; understanding of each other's sexuality; willingness to move forward with your mutual plans.

Oracle Blending two spirits is like pouring two waters into one glass, the fusion of two hearts is the true alchemy.

The Devil
Arcanum 15
Crystal: obsidian
Astro link: Capricorn

General keywords Financial or material temptation; be wary of power tripping from you or someone else; illusions about achievement; trapped by one's lifestyle; addictive behaviour.

Love keywords Don't be led astray by someone's power or money; confusing lust with love; falling in love too quickly without thinking of the consequences; seductive power or controlling behaviour.

Oracle The potency of love's magic is to share sexual expression, not possess it.

The Tower

Arcanum 16
Crystal: red agate
Astro link: Mars

General keywords Unexpected and sudden changes; disruptive influences; breakdown of the old to welcome the new; learning to adapt or adjust; falling apart to fall together again.

Love keywords A new challenge – either a new, unexpected romance, or a change in a relationship; whatever the case, welcome new challenges rather than avoiding them; an unwelcome intrusion in a love affair.

Oracle Order and chaos are inseparable. If lightning strikes, it will free you from restrictions; as the tower falls apart you also fall together.

The Star

Arcanum 17
Crystal: amber
Astro link: Aquarius

General keywords Creating your own opportunity; renewed self-belief; you can wish upon a star if you believe in it enough; being optimistic to succeed; realisation of a goal; financial or career achievement.

Love keywords Success in love; a romantic revelation will come to you in the nicest possible way; creative loving will lead to happiness, but are your expectations too idealistic?

Oracle Be a star. Light your own pathway to happiness and shine skywards, for all your hopes and dreams will come true.

The Moon
Arcanum 18
Crystal: aquamarine
Astro link: Pisces

General keywords All is not as it seems; use your intuition and instincts to guide you now; dishonesty in the workplace; being blind to the truth; unrealistic goals or dreams.

Love keywords A tricky love affair; are you deceiving yourself, or is someone deceiving you? Wrapped up in feelings or overthinking; be aware of what you truly feel in any new romance.

Oracle Trust in your intuition, not your imagination. The reflections you see are only the light in the mirror, not the truth behind that reflection.

The Sun
Arcanum 19
Crystal: clear quartz
Astro link: the sun

General keywords Positive energy; childlike fun; happiness and sharing; accomplished loving; creative togetherness; good communication.

Love keywords Liberated from relationship doubts and fears; a fulfilling relationship is about to begin; accepting someone for who they are; being in love and carefree.

Oracle The happiness you seek is yours to take. Create your own words of joy, and you create your own fabulous future.

Judgement
Arcanum 20
Crystal: amethyst
Astro link: Pluto

General keywords Being liberated from subjective opinions; re-evaluation and revival; dropping old values and embracing new ones; accepting things the way they are – there is no one to blame, not even yourself.

Love keywords Let go of the past and start afresh without feeling guilty; insight into how to best relate; free from scepticism about love; expressing opinion without being holier-than-thou.

Oracle We dance freely when we liberate ourselves from those worn-out beliefs; we dance wildly and in tune with ourselves when we transform doubt into certain success.

The World
   Arcanum 21
   Crystal: onyx
   Astro link: Saturn

General keywords Fulfilment, time for celebration; reward for hard work; success ahead; completion and freedom; the world is your oyster; going on a trip of a lifetime – whether literally or a new venture.

Love keywords You've met the ultimate love match; there's no turning back in a fabulous love affair; you can look forward to a fulfilling and creative relationship; romantic bliss.

Oracle Now you are one step nearer to your heart's desire. Now you are one step further from the chains of negativity.

Now we come to the Minor Arcana and its four suits of fourteen cards.

The Minor Arcana

As there are so many cards and not much space in this little book, here are brief keyword interpretations of each of the cards to get you started.

Wands

Wands are the cards of action. They are connected to the way we express ourselves, get things done, and interact with the world. They correspond to the fire signs – Aries, Leo and Sagittarius – in astrology.

Ace of Wands – new enterprise, creativity
Two of Wands – inspiration, achievement
Three of Wands – foresight, adventure
Four of Wands – celebration, freedom
Five of Wands – challenge, disagreement
Six of Wands – accomplishment, pride
Seven of Wands – defiance, purposefulness
Eight of Wands – re-evaluation, news
Nine of Wands – self-awareness, persistence
Ten of Wands – uphill struggle, burdened
Page of Wands – insight, messenger
Knight of Wands – impatience, impetuousness
Queen of Wands – self-assured, magnetic
King of Wands – masterly, charismatic

Cups

Cups are about our feelings and emotions. They show us how we deal on a deeper level with our relationships, and they correspond to the element of water in astrology. The water signs are Cancer, Scorpio and Pisces.

Ace of Cups – new love, expressing feelings
Two of Cups – romantic connection, new attraction

Three of Cups – abundant love, trusting others
Four of Cups – self-doubt, defensiveness
Five of Cups – disappointment, letting go
Six of Cups – playful feelings, sharing
Seven of Cups – too much choice, wishful thinking
Eight of Cups – moving on, starting anew
Nine of Cups – physical satisfaction, contentment
Ten of Cups – emotional happiness, completion
Page of Cups – sensitive lover, flirtatious admirer
Knight of Cups – emotional rescue, knight in
    shining armour
Queen of Cups – understanding, compassionate
King of Cups – security, wise judgement

Swords

Swords are about the way we think – specifically the way
our mind works, our fears, doubts and illusions. They also
remind us to work with the wisdom of the heart, not the
confusions of the mind. Swords relate to the element air in
astrology. The air signs are Gemini, Libra and Aquarius.

Ace of Swords – objectivity, facing the facts
Two of Swords – in denial, avoiding your emotions
Three of Swords – wounded, jealous thoughts
Four of Swords – contemplation, re-appraisal
Five of Swords – hollow victory, mental hostility
Six of Swords – new perspective, positive direction
Seven of Swords – self-deception, running
    from the truth
Eight of Swords – being powerless, self-sabotage

Nine of Swords – guilt, worry, sleepless nights
Ten of Swords – playing the victim or feeling
    vulnerable
Page of Swords – mentally alert, challenging lover
Knight of Swords – frank, incisive, impatient
Queen of Swords – astute, realistic, quick-witted
King of Swords – patriarchal but articulate

Pentacles

Also known as Discs or Coins, Pentacles are associated with the astrological element of earth. The earth signs are Taurus, Virgo and Capricorn. They describe the way we interact with the material or so-called tangible world, and also how we define or shape our lives accordingly.

Ace of Pentacles – prosperity, reward for effort
Two of Pentacles – flexibility, infinite possibilities
Three of Pentacles – proving oneself, skill and
    competence
Four of Pentacles – controlling, limited viewpoint
Five of Pentacles – unworthy, lack of control
Six of Pentacles – loss or gain, wielding power
    through giving
Seven of Pentacles – assessment, fruits of
    one's labour
Eight of Pentacles – self-discipline, dedication,
    perseverance
Nine of Pentacles – independence, self-reliance
Ten of Pentacles – wealth and material security
Page of Pentacles – focus, effort or good progress

Knight of Pentacles – persistence pays off, realistic contact

Queen of Pentacles – resourceful friend, warm-hearted and generous

King of Pentacles – reliable contact, financially savvy

Spreads

Although there are so many variations of these brief inter-pretations and positions in a spread or layout, the above brief guide will help you to understand their intrinsic meaning. Here are three easy spreads with example inter-pretations to get you going.

Layout 1: me, now and in the future

This layout will enable you to identify your current situation, your desires for the future, and what will actually be your next short-term gift from the universe.

1. Shuffle and choose three cards (see page 219 for suggestions on deciding on your method for choosing the cards), then place them face down in a line from left to right on a table or the floor in front of you.

2. When you have laid out the three cards, turn over the first card and interpret it. Then, similarly, turn over the second card and interpret it before you turn over the third card. This will help you to focus on each card in turn. As a beginner, seeing all three images, if turned over all

at once, before you try to interpret them, could put you off track.

Here is a brief example reading:

Position 1 – who I am right now (the present):
The Empress
Interpretation: right now, I am self-assured,
    confident about myself and my goals.

Position 2 – what I want in the future
    (my desire):
The Hierophant
Interpretation: I want to get to know someone who
    can be a mentor or teach me new skills.

Position 3 – the gift to me (the outcome):
Temperance
Interpretation: I will meet someone who will help
    me see from a new perspective, but I will have
    to moderate my plans or make compromises to
    get what I want.

Layout 2: making a decision

This is another simple layout using five cards to stretch your interpretive powers a little further. Again, shuffle and choose your cards as explained above. Draw one card at a time, think of what decision needs to be made right now, and lay the cards face down. The spread is in the shape of the points of a compass. Place card number 1 to the north, card number 2 to the south, card number 3 to the east, card number 4 to the west, and card number 5 in the middle. The cards represent the following:

1. You now
2. The key to making the right decision
3. Who is a good influence
4. Who is a negative influence
5. The outcome

Here is an example interpretation:

Position 1 – You now
Five of Cups
Interpretation: you are currently uncertain whether you should leave a difficult relationship and move on to find someone new.

Position 2 – The key to making the right decision
The Fool
Interpretation: the key to making the right decision is your ability to take a risk and to take a chance on a new romance.

Position 3 – Who is a good influence?
The Queen of Wands
Interpretation: a good influence would be a woman who understands the situation, who has perhaps been in the very same dilemma before.

Position 4 – Who is a negative influence?
The Page of Cups
Interpretation: the negative influence is a youth or
    younger man who won't have your best interests
    at heart, only his own.

Position 5 – The outcome
Nine of Pentacles
Interpretation: the outcome is that you will be
    freed from emotional baggage and feel liberated
    and independent.

Layout 3: what he thinks; what I feel

Lastly, here's a shortened version of one of my favourite
spreads using seven cards, where you can (as long as you
are totally objective) discover what your partner thinks
and feels about you, and vice versa. Shuffle and choose
your cards as explained above. Draw one card at a time,
think of what decision needs to be made right now, and
lay the cards face down as follows. Place the first six cards
in pairs to make two columns: card 1 to the left, card 2
to the right, card 3 to the left, card 4 to the right, and so
on. The column on the left represents you; the one on the
right represents him. Now place the final card centrally
above both columns.

7. The outcome

1. What he thinks about me	2. What I think about him
3. What he feels about me	4. What I feel about him
5. What he wants to happen to us	6. What I want to happen to us

Here is an example reading.

Position 1 – what he thinks about me
The Sun
Interpretation: he thinks you are witty, funny, great fun, and a joy to have around.

Position 2 – what I think about him
Knight of Swords
Interpretation: I think he's hard to pin down, very exciting and dynamic, but I'm not sure how much he cares.

Position 3 – what he feels about me
The Empress
Interpretation: he feels great warmth in my company and knows I am a woman he can trust.

Position 4 – what I feel about him
Six of Pentacles
Interpretation: I feel he wants to share more of his
  life with me.

Position 5 – what he wants to happen to us
Ace of Pentacles
Interpretation: He wants us to be together, but it
  could be more because of material or financial
  gain than true love.

Position 6 – what I want to happen to us
The Lovers
Interpretation: I want us to be the perfect loving
  couple, where romance and passion are more
  important than anything else.

Position 7 – The outcome
The Devil
Interpretation: The outcome is that we may
  both be bound by our own ideals, rather than
  accepting reality, so we must take care with
  our hearts.

Now that you have tried out a couple of basic spreads, you
can either create your own or look at many of the tarot
publications available to give you a diversity of ideas.

Why use the tarot?

Simply, the tarot is one of the most direct and insightful ways to see what is happening in your life right at this moment, and it also provides a vivid picture book of your past and future. Working with these incredible images reveals not only your own truth, but it also enables you to tap into your magical powers.

Remember: practice, intuition and trust that 'what you see before you reflects the truth of who you are' are the keys to working with the tarot to establish future trends and decisions in your life. With the tarot's help, you can seriously make destiny all your own.

Next, we come to one of the old-time favourites: the powerful symbols of the lines of our hands, and how this unique handprint is also a key to the kind of lifestyle that suits the core you.

Palmistry

Palmistry is simply the art of interpreting and reading the lines that criss-cross your palm, and sometimes also interpreting the shapes and lengths of hands and fingers. In a way, it's like reading a road map of your life journey that is dependent on your character (as is any fortune-telling or future prediction).

To do this, all you need is your own, or someone else's,

palm. Before you go off reading other people's hands, though, learn to read your own lines, and also remember the rules of divination as discussed on page 165. Of course, you also need to stick to a few tried-and-tested interpretative rules for the various lines and their meanings.

Hand shapes and palm lines are easily identifiable by the descriptions I have given below. When you meet someone for the first time, as on a romantic date, you can't exactly grab their hands and gaze at their palms to investigate their lines, but you can usually see the shape of their hands. It's a bit like reading body language, so observe discreetly and take note.

Hand shapes

There are four predominant hand shapes, which correspond (yes, magical correspondences at work again) to the four elements of astrology. These four shapes show the dominant traits of your character and future potential.

First, hold your major hand (your main writing hand) in front of you, palm facing. Look at the hand types outlined below to decide which shape your hand is most like. When looking at other people's hands (as on that first date) this is the simplest formula for getting a quick insight into the shape.

- Square-shaped palm with short or medium-length fingers
- Square palm with long fingers
- Long palm with short or medium-length fingers
- Long or slim palm with long or fine fingers

Earth hands
The square or practical hand:

Shape Square palm with shortish or thick fingers.

Dominant traits A loving, honest, hard-working attitude to life. You have down-to-earth common sense and a realistic approach to love. You are a great crafts person, and you excel in a team where you can put to use your creative talents.

Potential Work in a physical or active environment, close to nature, art or beauty to bring happiness into your life.

Fire hand
The active or intuitive hand:

Shape Medium-length   fingers   and   rectangular or long palm

Dominant traits Restless and lively, you thrive on challenge and adventure. Your self-motivation gets you places, but being provocative can lead to complex love affairs. You are best suited to working alone, or being the leader of the pack.

Potential You need a fast-paced, ever-changing career, which will showcase your vision of success.

Air hand
The balanced or intellectual hand:

Shape Square palm with long, fine fingers

Dominant traits With a brilliant mind, good logic and idealistic objectives, you are able to remain diplomatic and light-hearted in your career. Romantic and astute, you prefer an easy-going love life where you have an equal partner.

Potential You are best involved in media, communication work or researching some great new idea and making sure you learn something new every day.

Water hand
The sensitive or artistic hand

Shape Long, slim palm and long fingers

Dominant traits When the middle finger is longer than the length from base of palm to base of that finger, you may be the ultimate artistic genius. Otherwise, you are truly sensitive, psychic and intuitive. You're also the ultimate romantic, and can be gregarious one day, solitary the next, but always kind and gentle.

Potential Develop your artistic, musical or love-of-humanity skills and be rewarded. A little more self-love will enhance your relationships too.

The main palm lines

Here are the four main lines of the palm, a few variations of each, and some useful interpretations to get you started.

1. The life line This line starts above the thumb and either curves or runs straight down to the wrist. It usually starts about halfway between thumb and the joint of the first finger at the palm, just below the head line.

The life line reveals your life journey, your potential, the way you live, your vitality and sense of achievement. Variations are:

- Curves widely into the middle of the hand: independent, radical and a great traveller.
- Stays close to thumb: you prefer known surroundings, family values and a contented home life.
- Double life line (a parallel line close to the main life line): either you live a double life yourself – you live in two different countries, have two lovers, work in one job by day, another by night – or you have a twin or guardian angel on your side.

2. The heart line This line starts on the outside edge of your palm a few centimetres below your little finger and either curves or runs straight inwards across the palm, usually ending either just below your middle or first finger. This line describes your emotional and love life. Variations are:

- A strong, well-defined line: love relationships or romantic attachments are key themes in your life.
- Line very short, thin, weak or peters out: you're not really in touch with your feelings. Emotional involvement is less important to you than physical desire.
- Line ends in the middle of middle finger: you like to control the relationship, but you put your heart and soul into your love affairs. You are good at building long-term commitment.
- Line ends between first and middle finger: you are charismatic and passionate; you're highly seductive and love to be in love.

3. The head line This line starts between the thumb and first finger, and runs across the centre of the palm. It passes above the life line and ends below the heart line.

The line reveals your creative ability, career direction and your mental outlook on life. Variations are:

- A strong, wide line: a strong sense of duty, a methodical attitude and a willingness to get on with the job.
- A fine, faint or short line: difficulty in concentrating or making decisions.
- A long line that wraps right round to the outer edge of the palm: indicates that you can get lost in thought or talk over others.
- If the head line is joined to the life line: you have found it hard to free yourself from family

expectations. You were shy when young, but later you have compensated by becoming highly independent and realising your true talents.
- Line ends in a fork: this is a sign of communicative skills and talent in writing or other media careers.
- Line dips down towards the wrist: artistic and creative, you need to be on your own a lot to free up your powerful imagination.

4. The fate line The fate line starts from a point at the base of the middle of the palm, running up to the base of the fingers.

This line usually refers to your motivation, and attitude to ambition or goals. Variations are:

- Straight and strong: you know what you want and where you're going – and more importantly you know how to get it.
- Short and/or faint: you're not very ambitious and believe that others are often too obsessed with achievement. But you work well in a laid-back, low-pressure working environment with lots of friends or surrounded by animals.
- Breaks in the line: you have many changes of direction, and your motivation is scattered, but you're philosophical that success can come and go. You are extremely adaptable to changes in fortune.

Armed with some basic knowledge about reading palms,

you can now add a little more magic to your life and reveal the direction of your own future. Now let's look at another way to discover your potential, and how to augment the qualities you possess: numerology.

Numerology

Have you consistently found that one number seems to pop up in your life far more often than coincidence or chance might suggest? Perhaps you have always had a random series of similar phone numbers, or lived at the same street number or flat just by apparent chance? Every time you drive down the road, a car number plate might seem to always add up to the same single digit number? If so, then you have already noticed that numbers can be incredibly important to us. Numerology is the ancient art of divination based on the power of specific numbers. We are going to concentrate on the single digit numbers 1 to 9.

Pythagoras and vibrational energy

A long time ago, the 6th-century BCE Greek philosopher Pythagoras believed that numbers resonated to the vibrational harmonies of the universe. He wrote that 'numbers are the first things of all nature'.

The 'music of the spheres', as it was also called, was about sacred geometry, proportions and harmonic numbers, which resonated to the vibrational energy of the planets, the sky, stars and the cosmos, as it was then known.

The Pythagorean system is based on the nine primary numbers, and by working out your birth-date number and your relationship number, you will discover about your relationship style and main character traits. Like many other associations in this book, numbers play a key role in getting you in touch with your secret desires, destiny and personality; for example, it can help you to:

- find compatible partners, workplaces and addresses
- work out key dates for making decisions or arranging events
- reveal your secret desires
- change your name and destiny to suit you
- learn what challenges you need to overcome.

Your **relationship number** is calculated from the letters in your name. It describes your relationships and the way you interact with others.

Your **birth number** is calculated from your date of birth. This is a number that you can't change. It refers to your dominant character traits.

How to find your relationship number

Decide on the name you prefer to be called; for example, you might have been born with the name Anne Smith but you prefer to be called Annie or Anya, or even Jane! You might have a middle name that you don't like, but what is important is which name you prefer to be called by your family and friends. If you have married and changed your surname, use whichever name you feel most comfortable with. If you don't like your first name, or prefer a silly nickname, as long as it feels right for you, choose that name.

You can also work out your birth name and your current name and then check the difference (if there is one) and see if you've unconsciously changed your name to alter your life in some way, or to be different from the crowd.

Here is the alphabet code to work out your number.

1	2	3	4	5	6	7	8	9
a	b	c	d	e	f	g	h	i
j	k	l	m	n	o	p	q	r
s	t	u	v	w	x	y	z	

All you have to do is look down the columns to find the letters of your name, and see which number each letter corresponds to. Write them all down, then add up the numbers until you reduce the final number down to a digit between 1 and 9.

Here's an example based on the name Annie Smith:

$$A = 1, N = 5, N = 5, I = 9, E = 5, S =$$
$$1, M = 4, I = 9, T = 2, H = 8$$

Add these up and you get 49.

Now reduce this by adding them together: $4 + 9 = 13$.

Then reduce them again: $1 + 3 = 4$.

Annie Smith's **relationship number** is 4.

How to find your birth number

Using the same method, write down your date of birth in the following format: day, month (as DD/MM) and then the year in full (YYYY); for example 1 January 1984 would be 01 01 1984.

Here's an example based on a birth day of 14 February 1991:

$$1 + 4 + 0 + 2 + 1 + 9 + 9 + 1$$

Add these up and you get 27.

Now reduce this to one digit: $2 + 7 = 9$.

The **birth number** is 9.

Here's a run-down of the basic meanings of the nine numbers.

Number 1

Birth number Making an impact wherever you go, you're a born leader and need to be number one in everything. Independent and single-minded, you aim high and your pioneering spirit gets you results quickly.

Relationship number You're quick to fall in love or to make friends, but you don't like anyone getting too close to you. Romance matters, so do spontaneous encounters and hilarious conversations in and out of bed. Socially, you're really confident and attract an entourage of admirers in business or pleasure, but if you're not centre stage, you'll leave in a hurry.

Number 2

Birth number Calm, capable and cooperative, you're a born negotiator and are happy when everyone else is content and happy too. Emotionally sensitive, you sort out your friends and fix their relationship problems.

Relationship number In all affairs of the heart, you need emotional and physical closeness. Commitment is essential and you are traditional when it comes to long-term love and marriage. Although you're very protective, you can retreat into your shell when you feel threatened, and you need someone around who is as sensitive and caring as you are. Secretly looking for more romance? If your birth number or sun sign is more light-hearted, you'll have the perfect balance.

Number 3

Birth number You have a gift for words and your quick wits get you out of any difficult encounters. You prefer to travel light and not have anyone dependent on you, but as a great communicator you're bright, breezy and have a great sense of adventure.

Relationship number Life is for living to the full, and you're the ultimate social butterfly. The unpredictable is often preferable than the tried and trusted. Flirtatious and seductive, you can get led astray by a pretty face, but you always adore the one you're with, for however long! Constant? You? If your birth number is less flighty, or you have an earthy or fixed sun sign such as Taurus or Leo, love can be a true long-term commitment plus a laugh a minute.

Number 4

Birth number Organised and consistent, you are incredibly practical and have a strong sense of boundaries. Self-disciplined and strong-willed, you stick to your beliefs and are a trustworthy friend or colleague.

Relationship number Yes, even you need a certain amount of personal space or you feel like a poor bird trapped in a cage. In love, you swing between a secret desire for inciting a few emotional sparks and a love of peace. The good news is that if you are free to project-manage the practical aspects of the relationship, you will be the most loyal and true of partners.

Number 5

Birth number You thrive best with intellectual stimulation and personal freedom in bucket-loads. You want adventure, excitement, a versatile lifestyle and a jam-packed social life. In fact, the word 'routine' is taboo in your personal world, whereas curiosity, spontaneity, intrigue and wit are essential.

Relationship number You fall in love fast, and often have more than one admirer waiting in the wings, because you can see the talents and benefits of all kinds of different lovers. Witty, funny and great company, you can get bored easily and need a partner who likes variety, plenty of changing scenarios, and who also needs as much personal space as you do.

Number 6

Birth number With a laid-back, harmony-loving personality, you're happy to please others to keep the peace. A great diplomat, you are also able to see both sides of an argument, stay grounded and remain compassionate.

Relationship number A conventional loving relationship suits you best, where both of you are equal partners. Home and family matter, and you thrive in a peaceful, harmonious environment, where everything is in its place. Because you can't handle conflict, you tend to hide your head in the sand. This can make you resentful and/or partners distant, but if you have a fiery or airy sign, such as Sagittarius or Gemini, you'll be able to combine gentle loving with fun times, and an inspiring match.

Number 7

Birth number A self-reliant seeker of knowledge, you can appear to be absorbed in your personal world, preferring solitude and living close to nature. Inventive, spiritual and charming, you leave a lot to chance and don't make decisions easily; however, you're one of those people who seems to be born lucky.

Relationship number Idealistic about romance and the ideal soulmate, you find it hard to commit to one person, believing someone better will come along. But when in love you are charming, intuitive and sensitive, and love becomes all-encompassing, often taking over your whole life. Since you are not particularly materialistic or organised, when love starts to become routine, it can be disillusioning and you can feel let down, mostly because no human being can really live up to your lofty ideals.

Number 8

Birth number If you're not running a business, you'll be driven to succeed in some way. You're incredibly self-sufficient, and have to take control of every situation, but yet you often have a secret desire to forget the material world and get back to nature. Dogmatic at times, you find it hard to relax, but you never give up on a mission.

Relationship number Although you prefer working relationships to intimate personal ones, if you can combine the two, you could create a highly successful partnership. Although you can be a bit of a control freak, you're loyal and magnanimous when you know you can trust someone in your private world. Decisive and organised, you would also be the perfect power behind any lover's throne, until the time came to sit on your own throne too!

Number 9

Birth number Being so friendly and easy-going makes you a lot of friends and gets you places. You are humanitarian, caring and selfless, and a born campaigner. Adventurous and free-spirited, you are also highly creative and have a penchant for travelling light wherever you go in the world.

Relationship number Romantic and idealistic, you find it hard to commit to a long-term relationship, unless your partner is as independent as you are. You love the intrigue of secret love affairs, and this can get you tangled up in some clandestine love triangles. With your need for space and freedom you hate being pinned down. Stick to the open road with an equal free spirit, and you might just stick together for life.

Compatibility using numerology

Here's a quick-and-easy way to check who you get on with best:

1/1 – challenging but exciting
1/2 – sensual and indulgent
1/3 – playful but mischievous
1/4 – power players, yet dramatic
1/5 – creative and dynamic
1/6 – erratic, yet spicy
1/7 – escapist and unpredictable
1/8 – motivated but controlling
1/9 – spirited and adventurous

2/2 – friendly and productive
2/3 – unpredictable/sexy
2/4 – cosy and pragmatic
2/5 – focused and original
2/6 – calm, organised
2/7 – blow hot and cold
2/8 – ambitious, successful

2/9 – obstreperous but steamy

3/3 – light-hearted, easy
3/4 – happy-go-lucky, progressive
3/5 – wicked and hilarious
3/6 – communicative but disorganised
3/7 – romantic, carefree
3/8 – passionate yet thoughtful
3/9 – restless and impulsive

4/4 – calm, serene
4/5 – possessive but erotic
4/6 – organised and logical
4/7 – uneasy, suspicious
4/8 – solid, enterprising
4/9 – unpredictable, challenging

5/5 – harmonious, hilarious
5/6 – disorganised but original
5/7 – dreamy, easy-going
5/8 – sexy, indulgent
5/9 – inspirational, heavenly

6/6 – perfect, contained
6/7 – laid-back, supportive
6/8 – successful, dedicated
6/9 – companionable but argumentative

7/7 – soulmates, but unrealistic
7/8 – edgy, challenging

7/9 – creative, fascinating

8/8 – showy achievers
8/9 – challenging but short-lived

9/9 – intrepid, wild, reckless

Conclusion

Conclusion

You may have read this little book of practical magic out of curiosity or a desire to know yourself and the world of magic better. Whatever the reason, I hope that you have found it inspiring and want to try some of the techniques for yourself. Before you go off to make a magical life, however, let's return to Shakespeare's hubble-bubble witches in *Macbeth*, who, in the middle of some cauldron magic, sense that Macbeth is about to gate-crash their coven. One of them magically commands the doors to open to greet their intruder:

> '*Open, locks,*
> *Whoever knocks.*'

Whatever one might think of Macbeth as a character, to my mind this witchy line is a great analogy for welcoming magic into your life and to take charge of your destiny. If you've enjoyed this book, start putting the magic it encompasses into practice. Open the locks of disbelief, open yourself to the magic within you, and if you knock on the door with true integrity, trust, curiosity and *joie de vivre*, your life will be like that too: a magical place filled with all the harmonious delights of the universe.

Enjoy!

Conclusion

You may have read this little book of practical magic out of curiosity or a desire to know yourself and the world of magic better. Whatever the reason, I hope that you have found it inspiring and want to try some of the techniques for yourself. Before you go off to make a magical life, however, let's return to Shakespeare's hubble-bubble witches in *Macbeth*, who, in the middle of some cauldron magic, sense that Macbeth is about to gate-crash their coven. One of them magically commands the doors to open to greet their intruder:

> *'Open, locks,*
> *Whoever knocks.'*

Whatever one might think of Macbeth as a character, to my mind this witchy line is a great analogy for welcoming magic into your life and to take charge of your destiny. If you've enjoyed this book, start putting the magic it encompasses into practice. Open the locks of disbelief, open yourself to the magic within you, and if you knock on the door with true integrity, trust, curiosity and *joie de vivre*, your life will be like that too: a magical place filled with all the harmonious delights of the universe.

Enjoy!